THEY ASKED WHY

AND GOD

ANSWERED THEM

Bible people who asked God why
and the answers they received
with an emphasis on why there is suffering
if God is all good and all-powerful.

BY DR MARK C ROSER

UTTERMOST**MISSIONS**

Published by UM Publications

Published by Uttermost Missions Publishing
10300 Murdock Goshen Road
Loveland, Ohio 45140

They Asked Why: And God Answered Them by Mark C Roser (Bible people who asked God why and the answers they received with an emphasis on why there is suffering if God is all good and all-powerful). ·

Library of Congress Filing January 2024
ISBN: 978-0-9790009-1-1

2024 First Printing
Printed in the USA by
Morris Publishing®
3212 E. Hwy. 30
Kearney, NE 68847

All verses quoted from the New Kings James Version of the Bible unless otherwise noted, and italics in the quoted verses are the author's emphasis.

Available online at: www.mcroser.com
Pysical Copy, Digital, and Audio

Endnotes provided for references are found in the back of the book.

DEDICATION

They Asked Why is Dedicated to Ethan Andrew Roser.
You took me beyond what I knew to feel the heart of God.
God used you to change me in ways I could not imagine.
May I never stop changing until I see you again in glory.
May I never stop asking God for a thousand, thousand Ethans.

CONTENTS

APPENDIX

WHY
ASK WHY?

Larry King, a CNN talk show host, posed a favorite question during his interviews with famous people: "Why?"

He always homed in on that question to get to the heart of a person's story. "You changed your career!" Larry would ask, "Why?" The *why* question not only kept the conversation moving, but it also provided details on hidden reasons behind the facts.

Journalists know that every story is based on five W questions: who, what, when, where, and why. No story is complete without answers to these questions. Like the tragic news of yet another mass shooting, who was the shooter? What happened? When and where did it happen? How many were murdered? WHY?

"Why?" is the most elusive question of the five. Consider a recent headline: "Searching for a Motive: Police, FBI descend on home of suspected Texas shooter where he reportedly lived with parents."[1] The why question can lead to a host of other questions: Did the shooter target people they knew or shoot total strangers? Was it an act of terrorism? It takes time to get answers to "why?" It is easy to draw wrong conclusions, but invariably, we want to know "Why?" Merriam-Webster Dictionary defines why as "for what cause, reason, or purpose."[2]

WHY ASK WHY?

From infancy, answers to why questions empowered you to understand what you experienced. "Why did Mom look at me that way?" "Why should I do that?" "Why did that happen to me?" Although not consciously asked, why was a main avenue of learning and managing your various relationships and experiences. Later in life, many experience huge why questions: "Why is there something rather than nothing?" "Why am I here?" "Why do people suffer?"

The big questions of life have always drawn my attention. They helped bring me to faith in Christ when I was nineteen years old. They also helped me grow in my faith and motivated me to obtain a doctorate in Biblical Studies. They propelled me to write books on "What is the purpose of life?" "What can the Devil do, and why?" "What will happened when the world ends?"[3]

If you don't understand the reason for something, you're not sure how to think about it or how to respond. "Why am I going through this?" can be a nagging, unsettling question.

On the Saturday afternoon of April 22, 2017, the question of why became intensely personal and inescapable. I received a call that my youngest son, Ethan, was in an accident. An errant hammer, thrown during a track and field event, hit him in the head. "Your Son didn't make it to the hospital!"

After that call, I lay on the floor, weeping. "God, why allow me to be hurt like this?" For over twenty-two years in the wilds of Africa, God had always protected my family. I knew He could have easily prevented the accident. Nothing is too hard for him, and I believe this so deeply that I wrote a book discussing our experiences with God's Sovereignty during the Zimbabwe crisis. Lying on the floor that day with tears streaming down my face,

I said, "Lord, this boy would have served you for decades."
Ethan had already led several of his friends to Christ, and he
possessed the full skill set to be an outstanding minister. He had
every reason to live. I needed to know God's reason for allowing
Ethan's life to be cut short.

My "why?" question was also fueled by the fact that Ethan was
deeply committed to Christ. He was nineteen years old, unusually
trouble-free, and happy, and studying for the ministry. He had
an amazing bubbly personality.

The added irony was the random nature of the accident, which
the media called "a freak accident." The national media had
picked up the story of the accident. It resonated with people
because of Ethan's testimony and the nature of the accident, but
also because the accident happened at a premier Christian college
to a missionary family who had served God for decades in Africa.
My family and I were all interviewed. Millions of people heard of
Ethan's life, faith, and tragic death.

That first week after that phone call, I started writing. It was a
way to drain my ocean of pain and process my loss. Blindsided: A Journey from Tragic Loss to Triumph Love described my
raw feelings as I journaled my internal dialogue with God. Like
millions before me, I sought to understand why God allows such
tragedies.

When I began my deep dive into why, I had no idea how God
would answer my question. It was a unique journey of discovery,
a tangible tapestry of things I could see and touch, things Ethan
wrote to God, words I had written to him, and events far beyond
my ability to orchestrate. Looking back, I see that God carried me
along to write Blindsided for reasons greater than my grief. By
the time I finished the book, my wife summed up our yearlong
journey saying, "God has had an ongoing conversation with us."

Right after COVID, I finished writing and marketed Blindsided via a video trailer that raised the question of why God allows such losses. Millions viewed it on Facebook. Thousands responded with posts of their own, which granted me a unique opportunity to see a vast sea of pain beneath the surface of our comfortable culture. It was as if deep was calling to deep.

Multitudes asked the same "why?" question: "I asked God that question when our four-year-old grandson was air flighted to Children's Hospital.... He had a brain tumor.... He loved God. He talked about Jesus all the time. He could read and loved Bible stories. He loved going to church. He was extremely smart and loved everyone. I asked God why?"

It is not only the death of a loved one that provokes the "why?" question, but a host of other losses: "I was kidnapped, robbed, and raped off my university campus. I spent the last three months searching my heart as to why God would let this happen to me."

Many posts revealed that time does not diminish the loss, nor does it always heal: "Fifty years ago, our first-born son, twenty years old, was studying for the ministry in Bible College when a semi-truck ran a stop sign at 70 mph. Both he and his fellow student were killed instantly. He had a strong Christian testimony and was a talented singer and musician."

The Blindsided promotional video claimed that God had answered my "why?" question. The Facebook responses to my claim revealed several insights, but what surprised me the most was that eight out of ten Christians believe God does not answer our "why?" questions. Many believed it was wrong to ask:
- "I learned a long time ago to never question God."
- "My church upbringing taught you not to ask why."
- "I myself have never asked God why he does what he does, and I don't see myself now asking him, Why?"

- "We must bite our tongue."
- "Questioning why is contrary to our faith in God."
- "It is futile to ask why!"

Having catalogued the Facebook responses, here is a shortlist of the top reasons given as to why one should not ask God "why?":
- "Asking God why is akin to blaming Him."
- "It is the Devil, not God, who is responsible for these things."
- "We will only know when we get to Heaven."
- "God knows what's best for you."
- "We will never truly know why God allows bad things to happen to good people."
- "We must just trust God in all things!"

Some offered reasons why God isn't giving answers to our questions:
- "It would be too painful."
- "You couldn't understand it if he did."
- "It would not help you."
- "Answers don't bring the person back."

From the responses, it seems that people believe: "God is not telling, so don't ask." I call this the Christian version of "Don't Ask, Don't Tell," and I get it. Don't go there, and advise others not to go there, because if you do, you will get stuck in a place of hurt.

A percentage of Facebook responders admitted that they were stuck:
- "I have asked that question every day since May 2020."
- "I wonder why all the time. Why my baby had to die?"
- "My thirteen-year-old daughter asks me these questions all the time."

Worse still, Facebook users warned that asking why may give way to unbelief. Perhaps you will end up bitter toward God. There were also more pragmatic Facebook responses. A fair number acknowledged the need to ask, but they did not believe God gives a reason:

- "God knows we are going to question him because we are human and frail with limited understanding and see through a dark glass."
- "He remembers that we are dust."
- "He knows what we're thinking, and He isn't offended or surprised when we ask why."

Then there was an individual who claimed that God answered their why: "When my son died suddenly while on Spring break, God answered my cry and questions! It was a supernatural rescue for both my son and my family. He even gave me Scripture to show what happened and why.... He assured me that my son was with him because he called on Jesus! We were transformed by his death into new Spirit-filled people, never to be the same."

I found that the "why, God?" question touches a deep nerve in people, a nerve that runs through the body of believers. Little did I realize, however, that most people have grave misunderstandings of what the Bible teaches on asking God why, and that what they believe does not help them in their loss.

Why? Because believers silently struggle with painful losses, and not just a few fall away from faith because they've been told there are no answers. This response is unhelpful because the number one question that keeps unbelievers in unbelief is "why all the suffering?"

How should believers respond to this elephant in the room? Does the Bible fail to provide answers? Is the faith of Christ silent on the subject?

I would not choose to write on the "why, God?" question. When I wrote Blindsided, that was it. In time, though, I realized the need for a book that addresses this confusing subject because the Bible clearly speaks to our "why?" questions!

The word why appears over five hundred times on its pages. Those in the Bible who sought to follow God often asked it. We can learn a lot from them; what they recorded in the Bible promises to help us cooperate with God's purposes.

"For everything that was written in the past was written to teach you, so that through the endurance taught in the Scriptures and the encouragement they provide we might have hope" (Romans 15:4).

They Asked Why And God Answered Them considers every place in the Bible where the word why appears.[4] One instance is with Rebecca, Isaac's wife, who asked God why she experienced a troublesome pregnancy. *"But the children struggled together within her; and she said, 'If all is well, why am I like this?' So she went to inquire of the Lord" (Genesis 25:22).* God answered Rebecca. *"And the Lord said to her: 'Two nations are in your womb, two peoples shall be separated from your body; One people shall be stronger than the other, And the older shall serve the younger.' So when her days were fulfilled for her to give birth, indeed there were twins in her womb" (Genesis 25:23-24).*

They Asked Why focuses on eight specific Biblical characters who asked God big "why?" questions. Each chapter deals with a different person in the Bible and then examines the answers they received with a particular emphasis on the reason for human suffering. Readers will learn many helpful lessons from the characters' questions. You will also see that the Bible provides both general and specific answers to "why?" questions. At the end of each chapter, I highlight clear-cut "Principles of Asking Why," exploring how the characters' experiences and these principles might help you and I with our specific "why?" questions.

CHAPTER ONE

MOSES
WHY IN THE BEGINNING

Because life elicits questions which lead to answers
and stimulate growth in your understanding of God, people,
the world you live in, and His redemptive ways.

Websites that answer your W questions the who, what, when, where, and why enjoy many hits. Everything from experts to whoever wants to venture an answer powers these queries. But sites that handle "why?" questions often disclose debates. Just Google "Why is there something rather than nothing?" Page after page of URLs come up. Wikipedia, the free online encyclopedia, appears first: "This is a question about the reason for basic existence which has been raised or commented on by a range of philosophers and physicists."[5]

I'm not sure why Wikipedia has no reference to religionists, but Moses is the best person to start with on the question of existence. In the book of Genesis, Moses provides the most accepted answer to that basic "why?" *"In the beginning God created the Heavens and the earth" (Genesis 1:1)*. Like Moses, half the people alive today believe in a creator God, even in places where there are no Bibles.[6] *"For since the creation of the world His invisible attributes are clearly seen, being understood by the things that are made, even His eternal power and Godhead" (Romans 1:20)*.

You and I are hard-wired to know right from wrong, to see beauty and design, to feel awe and wonder, and, ultimately, to seek the reason for things.[7] Genesis teaches that God made us that way in his own image and likeness. The word *genesis* means beginning, and all the major teachings of the Bible, from creation to redemption, from the justifying faith of Abraham to the redemptive suffering of the Promised Messianic Seed, have their roots in the first book of the Bible. Seeing how the "why?" question is used by Moses in the Torah will help you understand what Scripture teaches elsewhere this topic.

In Genesis, the question of why is often asked. In fact, Moses enters the Biblical narrative when he stops and asks "why?" *"Then Moses said, 'I will now turn aside and see this great sight, why the bush is not consumed'" (Exodus 3:3)*. Dry bushes in the wilderness heat up under the hot sun and burst into fiery flames. They are quickly consumed into oblivion. Moses had seen this happen many times on that mountainside. His whole life, he had started fires and watched how they burned twigs, to cook, to stay warm, and to get rid of the garbage, So, a bush on fire that did not burn up was hard to ignore! Moses had to find out why. *"When he turned aside to see that great sight, God called to him from the midst of the bush and said, "Moses, Moses!"* (Exodus 3:4).

A holy fire appeared to Moses on Mount Horeb, and in an upper room, a similar divine fire appeared to the first group of Jesus's followers. The latter got the attention of a multitude in Jerusalem as they heard in their native languages the marvelous works of God. *"So they were all amazed and perplexed, saying to one another, 'Whatever could this mean?' Others mocking said, 'They are full of new wine'"* (Acts 2:3-13).

Whole nations, not just individuals, can observe these deific occurrences.[8] Yet, they are mostly subtle, unspectacular, and appear as coincidences. For example, consider the American experience of the coincidental deaths of Thomas Jefferson and John Adams on July 4, 1826. The pair died fifty years to the day after each had signed the Declaration of Independence. They died in different places and from different causes. Add to this quirk occurrence that the U.S. president at the time was Adams's son John Quincy.[9]

LIFE INVARIABLY ELICITS QUESTIONS

God has a way of getting your attention. You experience something outside the norm, something unusual, or something where an unseen hand is apparent. Call it serendipity, or synchronicity; call it what you want. Something strange, something other-worldly, happens. It's God's calling card; it bears his fingerprints. It stirs you to ask why and to seek answers.

God alone can give true answers, which will keep you from scoffing at what is holy, like some did that first Pentecost!

- **You ask others "why?" to know their motives and purposes.**

You can ask God "why?" just like you might ask others why they do what they do. You see this kind of asking often in Genesis. *"Pharaoh called Abram and said, 'What is this you have done to me? Why did you not tell me that she was your wife? Why did you say, 'She is my sister'? I might have taken her as my wife. Now therefore, here is your wife; take her and go your way"* (Genesis 12:18-19; 29:25).

You especially want to know why when you witness strong emotions in others. *"So he asked Pharaoh's officers who were with him in the custody of his lord's house, saying, 'Why do you look so sad today?'"* (Genesis 40:7; 43:6; 44:4-7).

"Why did you say that?" "Why did you do that?" Starting in Genesis and throughout the Bible, people ask why. Even God asks people why. *"The Lord said to Abraham, 'Why did Sarah laugh, saying, 'Shall I surely bear a child, since I am old?'"* (Genesis 18:13).

When God asks a question, however, it is not to get information or gain an insight. He already knows why, but he asks so that you might get in touch with the seriousness of the moment. *"So the Lord said to Cain, 'Why are you angry? And why has your countenance fallen?'"* (Genesis 4:6).

- **God wants you to inquire of him as to the "why?" of what you experience.**

In Moses' inspired account of the patriarchs' lives, he doesn't hesitate to record their "why?" questions for God. Before Isaac was born, Abraham asked God why he had no heir. Also, Jacob wondered why *"everything is against me?!"* (Genesis 15:1-5; 42:1-36).

Moses followed the example of his forefathers and asked God why he didn't do what he had promised. Here's the storyline. God told Moses that he appeared to Abraham, Isaac, and to Jacob as God Almighty, and he hadn't forgotten his covenant to give them the land of Canaan. He heard the groaning of the children of Israel and saw how the Egyptians enslaved them. God promised to rescue them with an outstretched arm. But from the time God reiterated his promise to deliver them, their bondage went from bad to worse. The Egyptians increased the Israelites' workload and started beating their workers. *"So Moses returned to the Lord and said, 'Lord, why have You brought trouble on this people? Why is it You have sent me?'"* (Exodus 5:22).

- **The "Why?" question helps you learn God's ways.**

Moses is a notable example of a person growing closer to God and learning his ways because he asked God why. He was not afraid to ask God why he had not fulfilled his promise to rescue Israel. It was a bold question! But it was legit.

Have you ever been there? God promises healing, but you or your loved one gets sicker.... You believe God called you to start your business, but there's one setback after another.... God calls you to peace in a vital relationship, maybe at work or in your marriage, but strife is a daily reality.... You might have your list of "why?" questions. At times, Bible promises, and heartfelt dreams appear to fail like they did with Moses and the Israelites. It is part of the faith landscape of walking with God. Many of the heroes of our faith "died not having received the promises" (Hebrews 11:13).

RETURN OF THAT INITIAL GOD MOMENT

God gives Moses a clear answer as to why he hasn't delivered Israel yet. *"You shall know that I am the Lord"* (Exodus 6:7).

He reiterates that purpose *(Exodus 7:17:8:22; 11:7)*. It is a mega truth taught throughout Scripture. God does what you cannot do! The result is that you know it is God at work and not you. Otherwise, you might think you did it yourself, like when God reduced Gideon's army to three hundred. *"'Lest Israel claim glory for itself against Me, saying, 'My own hand has saved me'"* (Judges 7:2).

Salvation from sin, God's gift of eternal life, and your own existence are not things you brought about or achieved by your own doing. They are the work of God. The realization of this truth that it is Almighty God at work equals "You shall know that I am the Lord" (Exodus 16:6,12;31:13).[10] That is how you came to know his existence. "Know that the LORD, He is God; It is He who has made us, and not we ourselves; We are His people and the sheep of His pasture" (Psalm 100:3).

"You shall know the Lord" when you realize it is he alone who did something for you that you could not do alone. Often, it is best realized after you have expended your own efforts, tried, and failed, God shows up! It is how we come to know the Lord in all areas of your life. But it takes humility to truly acknowledge him and to receive what he offers. To often, this kind of knowing necessitates pain.

Answers to "why?" questions have helped me overcome disappointment, hurt, and confusion in order to follow Christ more closely. *My African Dream* tells my family's story of the death and resurrection of our vision to do mission work in Africa. My wife and I narrate our twenty-two years of work in Zimbabwe and the many answers we received to our questions. But better than my story, God has recorded how he answers his people in the Bible.

So, let's follow Moses and God around in the wilderness and see what we can learn from the "why?" questions that he asked God.

- **Why question helps you grow in intimacy with God.**

Moses came to know the LORD when he asked to see God's glory. (*Exodus 33:17-20*). The revelation of God's glory transformed Moses' life and ministry as he learned who God is, what God does, and why God works the way he does. The Lord is *"merciful and gracious, long suffering, and abounding in goodness and truth, keeping mercy for thousands, forgiving iniquity and transgression and sin, by no means clearing the guilty"* (Exodus 34:6-7).

Referred to in the Old Testament as the credo of who God is, and repeated often, the Psalmist says, *"The Lord executes righteousness And justice for all who are oppressed. He made known His ways to Moses, His acts to the children of Israel. The Lord is merciful and gracious, Slow to anger, and abounding in mercy. He will not always strive with us, nor will He keep His anger forever. He has not dealt with us according to our sins, Nor punished us according to our iniquities. For as the heavens are high above the earth, So great is His mercy toward those who fear Him"* (Psalm 103:6-11).

The entire theology of the Bible is built on this edifice of God's character, revealed in both his tender mercies and acute justice. *"Behold therefore the goodness and severity of God"* (Romans 11:22). To Moses, God went on to say, *"By no means clearing the guilty, visiting the iniquity of the fathers upon the children and the children's children to the third and the fourth generation"* (Exodus 34:7).

Moses became God's lawgiver, and you cannot appreciate the Old Testament without an appreciation of the rigors of God's law. Under the law, you see the severity of God. The law's rigid moral economy helped answer one of the biggest questions Moses and readers of the Old Testament ask: *"Then Moses pleaded with the Lord his God, and said: 'Lord, why does Your wrath burn hot against Your people whom You have brought out of the land of Egypt with great power and with a mighty hand?'"* (Exodus 32:11).

- Why questions help you understand hard truths like God's wrath against sin.

In reading the Old Testament, I've asked: "Why does God get angry?" The answer is clear: God's anger is the result of his holy love that hates sin because it destroys what he created. Before the Great Deluge, God's heart was full of pain because the earth was full of wickedness and violence *(Genesis 6:5-6)*. Man had defiled and destroyed most of the beauty God had created, but the floodwaters of judgement washed the earth and cleansed it of its unholy inhabitants.

Later, when Israel sinned, God's anger was kindled, but Moses pleaded with God to relent.[11] His rational appeal was based on what the Egyptians and other nations would think if God did not do what He promised: to bring the Israelites into the Promised Land. *"Why should the Egyptians speak, and say, 'He brought them out to harm them, to kill them in the mountains, and to consume them from the face of the earth'?"* *"Because the Lord was not able to bring this people to the land which He swore to give them, therefore He killed them in the wilderness" (Exodus 32:12-14; Numbers 14:12-16).*

Based on God's revealed nature, Moses interceded: *"Pardon the iniquity of this people, I pray, according to the greatness of Your mercy, just as You have forgiven this people, from Egypt even until now."* God listened to Moses and did what he asked. *"I have pardoned, according to your word" (Numbers 14:17-25).*

It is evident that God desired to keep his promises and not be misunderstood. It is also clear that Moses' intercession, which involved questions, was effective. Moses talked to God like a friend, and God answered him. But should you expect God to speak to you like Moses? Well, Jesus said that John the Baptist was greater than any of the prophets: *"But he who is least in the Kingdom of God is greater than John" (Luke 7:28).*

- **Why questions show openness and honesty in a relationship.**

As Moses' relationship with God grew, he was not afraid to ask for better working conditions, because Israel's unbelief not only provoked God to anger but also made life miserable for Moses. His appeal was extremely intense and personal. *"So Moses said to the Lord, 'Why have You afflicted Your servant? And why have I not found favor in Your sight, that You have laid the burden of all these people on me? Did I conceive all these people? Did I beget them, that You should say to me, 'Carry them in your bosom, as a guardian carries a nursing child,' to the land which You swore to their fathers?"* (Numbers 11:11-12).

God was not put off by Moses' tone. And the man wasn't finished. He raised his appeal to the nth degree, the nuclear option, asking God to kill him on the spot if that was how he would to treat him. *"Where am I to get meat to give to all these people? For they weep all over me, saying, 'Give us meat, that we may eat.' I am not able to bear all these people alone.... If You treat me like this, please kill me here and now'"* (Numbers 11:13-14).

- **The "Why?" question helps you learn God's ways.**

We could get the wrong impression of Moses if we did not know that he was *"the meekest man on earth"* (Numbers 12:3). Pride had nothing to do with Moses' questions. Nor was this a matter of personal temperament or spiritual immaturity. God answered Moses again and raised up seventy men of the elders of Israel to help him bear the burden of the people so that Moses did not bear it alone *(Exodus 11:16-17)*.

Moses' questions helped him avoid ministry burnout. For forty years, he patiently endured far more troubles and criticism from those he led than any pastor I know, yet he never gave up. He continued to lead God's people to the Promised Land, although he himself was not allowed to enter. God told him why, and Moses told the people it was their fault. *"Because of you the Lord became angry with me also and said, 'You shall not enter it, either'"* (Deuteronomy 1:37 NIV).

MOSES
ASKING GOD WHY

- Asking God why is encouraged for all the above introductory reasons and those reasons could be listed here. (Each ensuing chapter will list new principles based on the Bible character's experiences with God).
- Asking God why is an honest, legitimate question.
- Asking God why is based on a relationship with God in which we have demonstrated that we are committed to know and do his will at a cost to ourselves.
- Asking God why can be an act of faith as in Moses' case, or as with Israel, it can be an expression of disbelief, which reveals a lack of relationship with God.

There is a final vital point which Moses' questions clearly teach. There are wrong ways to ask God why. The Israelites are an example of how not to ask God why, and the hurt that brings. It is crucial to emphasize the glaring contrasts between Moses asking God why compared to the Israelites' question.

Five Contrasts:

1. Moses asked questions because he believed God. The Israelites questioned God out of doubt and unbelief.

The Israelites asked, *"Why has the Lord brought you to this land to fall by the sword, that our wives and children should become victims? Would it not be better for you to return to Egypt?"* (Numbers 14:3).

Unbelief is at the heart of the Israelites' questions, and their unbelief becomes a pattern in the wilderness. That generation did not enter the rest ordained for them, *"Because they did not believe in God, and did not trust in His salvation"* (Psalm 78:22). You might even label their question not a question at all, but a rhetorical voicing of unbelief, or, in other words, speaking against and challenging the person questioned. "The people spoke against God and against Moses: *'Why have you brought you up out of Egypt to die in the wilderness? For there is no food and no water, and our soul loathes this worthless bread'"* (Numbers 21:5).

2. Moses sought to cooperate with God's purposes in contrast to the Israelites, who resorted to open, vocal rebellion against God's good purposes for them.

The Israelites saw the plagues on the Egyptians, the death of Egypt's firstborn, the parting of the Red Sea, the destruction of Pharoah's army, and they ate manna from heaven and drank water from the rock. Although they saw many works of God, they failed to trust and obey. The result: they did not know the Lord, or learn his ways, or grow closer to him. Instead, Scriptures says, *"They always go astray in their heart, and they have not known My ways"* (Hebrews 3:10). Their rebellion was so bad they wandered for forty years in the wilderness. Unbelief can cause a person or group to not receive what God has promised. It is a main reason, as you'll see later, why God's promises remain unfulfilled.

3. Moses learned God's ways from the answers God gave, but the Israelites rejected God's answers, so they never learned how God would work out his salvation for them.

When God told them why he took them into the wilderness, they acted as if he was unworthy of their trust, and even a liar. They grumbled against God and Moses, and said, *"But you have led us into this wilderness to make this whole assembly die of famine!"* (*Exodus 16:3*). They consistently drew wrong conclusions and erred in their hearts. Their wilderness experience was meant to humble them for their good, to teach them that man does not live by bread alone, to introduce them to a new way of living, and to train them in reliance on God. But they refused to humble themselves and failed to trust that God's ways were best, which led to their progressive disobedience. Their rebellion reached a climax when the twelve spies returned with an evil report, and the whole nation sided with them. They did not believe God would bring them into the Promised Land. They held to their own hurtful thoughts and ways, and in their pride, they despised being dependent on God.

4. Moses knew the Lord as good and gracious character, but the Israelites spoke and acted as if God was evil, and they demanded that the Glorious, Self-Existent Lord of Creation justify his ways to his sinful creatures.

Questions are wrong when they are motivated by unbelief, when they reject God's ways, when they act as if God has no right to rule, when they think man's thoughts and ways are best, and when they believe God has evil motives. Such questions are asked in a perverse spirit. When you refuse to walk in God's ways, when you refuse to accept the answer he gives, when you do not expect God to do you good, your questions are an affront to God's character. This brings up a fifth contrast between Moses and the Israelites.

5. Moses in faith submitted to God's ways, whereas Israel in unbelief denied his rightful rule, which led to treason.

Paul confronted this type of insubordination: *"You will say to me then, 'Why does He still find fault? For who has resisted His will?' But indeed, O man, who are you to reply against God? Will the thing formed say to him who formed it, 'Why have you made me like this?' Does not the potter have power over the clay, from the same lump to make one vessel for honor and another for dishonor?"* (Romans 9:19-21).

Paul maintained that (1) God suffers long with rebels like he did with Pharoah, a type of Satan, who refused to submit to God and rather chose to do evil.[12] (2) God will reveal his power over evil in dealing with evildoers, demonstrating his glorious ability to work even their evil actions for good. (3) God will at the same time display his displeasure in judging them as an example to warn others, and (4) God will cut short their rebellion to bring about a lasting good for those who trust him *(Romans 9:12-24)*.

MOSES' "WHY?" SUMMARIZED

From the beginning of history, people have asked "why?" We long to understand the cause and reason for what we see and experience. Moses saw a bush on fire and had to find out why it didn't burn up. Moses often asked God "why?" questions, and God was not offended. Moses asked questions in faith to cooperate with the Lord's purposes. His questions are powerfully contrasted to the Israelites who asked God why in unbelief and only sought what they wanted.

Moses received answers and learned God's ways, Questions properly asked bring insights into who God is, what he does, and how he does it. Therefore, it is not wrong to ask God why in a humble attitude that seeks to serve him with understanding.

God promises to bring about good no matter what we face, provided we are willing to accept whatever answers he gives, even when we don't like our current circumstances and challenges.

You can, however, also appeal to God for changes in your present situation like Moses did. God always answered Moses, even when his answer was no you will go into the Promised Land. You will only see from the mountain top.

CHAPTER TWO

HABAKKUK
FAITH SEEKS ANSWERS

Because of God's attributes and the nature of Biblical faith,
which asks a sovereign God "why?" while believing that
He is good, regardless of what happens and how He answers.

Children ask lots of questions. Like thirsty learning sponges, they soak up everything around them, and their questions show that their brains and analytical skills are developing. Answered questions help them in many ways: understand the world they live in, overcome their fears, appreciate the benefits of relating to others, delay self-gratification, and learn new things, which stimulate ongoing growth. Studies prove that asking questions increases a child's desire to read and improves their communication skills.

The adults closest to a child are always their first choice for answering questions, but this can be exhausting for a mom and dad. Some parents thus discourage their children from asking them questions, but then they miss out on the benefits of these conversations. And would mom or dad want to entrust their child's questions to a stranger?

The prophet Habakkuk, like a child, asked God one question after another about the things he saw. In his first two chapters, a dozen question marks appear. As a result, Habakkuk has been called "A Book of Questions."[13] It is like the prophet interviewed God on current events that troubled him, and he did not avoid the difficult question of why God allowed such things to happen.

Background and Relevence

Habakkuk's strong relational faith prompted him to know God's purposes for his life in his day. The Book of Habakkuk thus reveals several vital truths of asking God why in order to serve him better. The answers God gave Habakkuk will also help you understand what the Almighty is doing today in your world and what he expects of you, especially when evil seems to triumph.

Reading the news can take on a whole new dimension, and fuel your prayer life. It certainly did that for the prophet Habakkuk.

Habakkuk lived in the Kingdom of Judah in 612 BC. Little is known about him beyond what we read in the book that bears his name. Unlike other prophets, he does not disclose his hometown, his occupation, or information concerning his parentage or tribe. It is as if those details are inconsequential; he could be any believer who has ever lived.

We know it was an evil time. Although Habakkuk had a strong faith in God, he struggled to reconcile his faith in God with the evil he saw all around him. He watched people break God's commands, commit violent crimes, practice deception, and rob and persecute the righteous. All the injustices he saw burdened him deeply, so he cried out to God.

Here are his initial questions for God: *"The burden which the prophet Habakkuk saw. O Lord, how long shall I cry, And You will not hear? Even cry out to You, 'Violence!' And You will not save. Why do You show me iniquity, And cause me to see trouble? For plundering and violence are before me; There is strife, and contention arises. Therefore, the law is powerless, And justice never goes forth. For the wicked surround the righteous; Therefore, perverse judgment proceeds"* (Habakkuk 1:2-4).

Habakkuk's question is no different from our question today: Why does an all-powerful and all- good God allow evil and the suffering that accompanies it? This question has troubled mankind for ages. C.S. Lewis, the famous Christian apologist, said, "The problem of pain is atheism's most potent weapon against faith in God. People point to this problem of evil as their reason more than any other for not believing in God. It is not merely a problem; it is the problem."[14]

The atheistic rationale argues that "either God is all-powerful but not all good, and therefore he doesn't stop evil—or he's all good but not all powerful, and therefore he can't stop evil."

Their third option is that "God simply doesn't exist." Their first two options are actually thier logic to arrive at the atheistism, and it is how they answer the problem of evil.

During the God is Dead movement, on July 12, 1968, there appeared on the cover of Life Magazine the horrifying photographs of starving children in war torn Biafra, Nigeria. Their bodies were skin and bones, like the bodies in Holocaust concentration camps. You've seen them. A young man, distraught by what he saw, took the magazine to a local pastor, and said, "Doesn't God know about this?" The pastor chided him for his question. The young man walked out of church to never return.

It is not, however, just atheists who struggle with the problem of evil. A recent Barna Poll asked people, "If you could ask God one question, and you knew he would give you an answer, what would you ask?" The most common response was "Why is there pain and suffering in the world? Why the tragedies and losses, the crimes, and injustices?"[15]

The question of suffering will eventually arise if you talk long enough to people about God. What answer do you give them? What answer do you give yourself when you suffer?

"Why God allows suffering" is not a mere theoretical question. It is very personal, intense, and specific: "Why did my dad die of Covid?" "Why did that tornado touch down here?" "Why did my child die in a car accident?" "Why was our child born with a disability?" "Why do I suffer with chronic pain?" "Why have my children gone astray?" The painful list seems endless.

In each life, rain falls, but a sprinkle can become a torrential downpour. You can't help but ask why? You ask, not in unbelief like the Israelites, but in genuine faith like Moses and Habakkuk. Will God answer you? How might his answer help you?

Like God answered Moses, let's see how he answers Habakkuk: *"Look among the nations and watch—Be utterly astounded! For I will work a work in your days Which you would not believe, though it were told you. For indeed I am raising up the Chaldeans, A bitter and hasty nation Which marches through the breadth of the earth, To possess dwelling places that are not theirs. They are terrible and dreadful... They all come for violence...They deride every stronghold, For they heap up earthen mounds and seize it"* (Habakkuk 1:6-10).

The all-knowing Lord knew precisely what was happening in the nation. He saw it all, even the thoughts and intents of people's hearts behind their evil actions. He told Habakkuk he would address the wickedness and even told him how he would do it. God would use the Chaldeans to judge King Jehoiakim's evil and the Judahites who broke his commands and mistreated their countrymen. The Chaldeans would invade the Judahites' land, and people would reap what they sowed.

Habakkuk understood that judgement begins in the house of God (*Leviticus 18:28; 1Peter 4:7*). God's answer of punishment, however, was more troubling to Habakkuk than the evil he saw in Judah, which had provoked his question for God in the first place. Simply put, in the prophet's estimation, the cure was worse than the disease. He could not understand how the Holy One of Israel could use such a wicked nation as Babylon and the Chaldeans as an instrument to judge his own.[16]

So, Habakkuk's first question led to a follow-up question, which was more desperate, direct, and bold than his first question: *"Are You not from everlasting, O Lord my God, my Holy One? We shall not die. O Lord, You have appointed them for judgment; O Rock, You have marked them for correction. You are of purer eyes than to behold evil And cannot look on wickedness. Why do You look on those who deal treacherously, And hold Your tongue when the wicked devours A person more righteous than he? Why do You make men like fish of the sea...*

*They catch them in their net, And gather them in their dragnet. There-
fore, they rejoice and are glad" (Habakkuk 1:12–15).*

Habakkuk basically said, "I'm shocked at your approach. Lord.
This is not right!" The prophet gave his shortlist of reasons: (1)
Because the Babylonians would surely harm the righteous Judahites alongside the wicked, just as the fisherman brings in a full
catch of both good and bad fish with his net. (2) Besides that,
even the wicked in Judah were not as wicked as the Babylonians.
(3) The kicker is that the Babylonians would credit their false
gods for their victory. It would be like God using the Russians
or Chinese to bring judgement on the United States for its sins,
while they ridicule the faith and freedoms of Americans.

Habakkuk, as Moses had, upped the stakes for God. He asked,
*"Are You not from everlasting?" Aren't you the I AM that I AM? Am I
mistaken about your nature and attributes? Aren't you all powerful?"*
In the next breath, he says, *"O Lord my God, my Holy One. Aren't you all
good?"* And Habakkuk wasn't done. He virtually demanded an answer:
*"I will stand my watch And set myself on the rampart, And watch to see
what He will say to me, And what I will answer when I am corrected"*
(Habakkuk 2:1).

Imagine saying to God, "I'm just going to stand here and wait
until you answer me." I don't know about you, but that strikes
me as either strong faith or foolish presumption. But it could
never be called unbelief.

Habakkuk was relentless even when he expected God to scold
him. Amazingly, God did not correct him. God again answered.
For Habakkuk sought to understand God's ways and cooperate with his purposes. The prophet's questions led him to fulfill
his ministry of admonishing sinners and warning the righteous
to flee for refuge. God assured Habakkuk that all sin would be
judged, but that judgement would begin in God's house.

Judah would be disciplined, and wicked Babylon later destroyed. Babylon's cruelty during the siege of Jerusalem would doom their fate. Nothing would be missed by God.

For you, like Habakkuk, the answer might not unfold the way you think it should or according to your timeframe. You might think it is slow in coming, but even if it seems to linger, wait for it. It will come. "Trust me on that," God says to his people.

"Then the Lord answered me and said: 'Write the vision And make it plain on tablets, That he may run who reads it. For the vision is yet for an appointed time; But at the end it will speak, and it will not lie. Though it tarries, wait for it; Because it will surely come, It will not tarry. 'Behold the proud, His soul is not upright in him; But the just shall live by his faith'" (Habakkuk 2:2-4).

God revealed the essential virtue to staying afloat and navigating amidst all the depravity, discipline, and destruction. Habakkuk and you and I who desire to be right with God need to trust God. In contrast, proud, self-reliant people trust in themselves to work things out. The Lord, however, provided not only the prophet, Judah, and us with that answer but all who would ever live. It's the most profound answer for properly living in a sinful world: *"But the righteous will live by his faith"* (Habakkuk 2:4). That answer is the main message found in Habakkuk and revealed elsewhere in Scripture. It's the saving response for rescue from this evil world.

In this broken world, you and I can live by faith in God. What a most awesome revelation Habakkuk's question brought: To be in right standing before a Holy, Almighty God, you must live by faith in him and not by what see in your passing circumstances. The answer "But the righteous shall live by faith" became the apostle Paul's clarion call for our response to the good news of Christ. Paul quotes Habakkuk in three places in the New Testament, and he brings out the full intent of those words:

"For there'n 's the r'ghteousness of God revealed from fa'th to fa'th: as 't 's wr'tten, 'The just shall l've by fa'th'" (Romans 1:17)

"But that no man is justified by the law in the sight of God, it is ev'dent: for, 'The just shall l've by fa'th'" (Galat'ans 3:11)

"'Now the just shall l've by fa'th' but 'f any man draw back, My soul shall have no pleasure 'n h'm" (Hebrews 10:38)

Aren't you glad Habakkuk asked? His questions led to a truly life-giving answer of faith. That answer confirmed the foremost response God requires for you to be saved. Trust in him.
It's not what you do such as keeping certain rules. It's what God does! But that kind of trust wasn't something new. It was what Abraham, the father of Habakkuk's faith, discovered generations earlier. Faith pleases God and if you put your trust in what God did in Christ, he imputes righteousness to your account. God is not a respecter of persons, but a respecter of those who put their trust in him. What he did for Abraham and Habakkuk, he will do for you and me.

Habakkuk understood God's answer, and it turned him from prophet into poet. He ended his two chapters of questions with a third chapter: an "All-in Faith-in God" song that is to be accompanied by a full orchestra of dancing worshippers. *"Though the fig tree should not blossom, nor fruit be on the vines, the produce of the olive fail and the fields yield no food, the flock be cut off from the fold and there be no herd in the stalls, yet I will rejoice in the LORD; I will take joy in the God of my salvation. GOD, the Lord, is my strength; he makes my feet like the deer's; he makes me tread on my high places. To the choirmaster: with stringed instruments" (Habakkuk 3:17-19).*

Things might make no sense. Your life may appear to go wrong. What do you do? Keep trusting! If circumstances remove the tangible things in life and there are no plants or animals to eat, still, you can rejoice in the Lord and not waver in your faith. Come what may, you can rejoice in God your Savior, even before you see any changes take place. You can rejoice because, although there are many things beyond your control, there is nothing outside his control. God will soon intervene and work it all out.

At the right time, God demonstrated his love by fully intervening in the affairs of mankind via Christ's incarnation, crucifixion, and resurrection. Because God became a human person lto die in your place for your sins and to rise from the grave for your justification, you can live joyfully, knowing your spirit has eternal life now. God will see your body and soul through the up and downs of living during this present evil age *(Romans 8:31-32)*.

You can trust God when your own life or nation is in turmoil. You can trust him when your enemy is striking out against you with all the evil he can muster. God has allowed it for a redemptive purpose, and his life-giving answer will move you not to distrust but to a firmer faith in him than you had before the test. It will move you from your burdens to his promises, from being perplexed to praising God, from confusion to unshakable confidence, and from anxious worry to one of the highest forms of possible worship, the sacrifice of praise.

The Bible provides many instances where God's people move from hurtful experiences to a place of great faith, even before they experienced what was promised. Hannah is noteworthy because for years her adversary had taunted her because she had no children, especially when she visited the temple at Shiloh. Her enemy gave her malicious answers as to why she didn't have children: *You don't deserve children. You don't have enough faith* or the subtle deceit of *it must not be God's will for you to have children (see 1 Samuel 1:6)*. However, when Hannah heard God's answer to her dilemma, she immediately responded in faith The priest Eli said, *"Go in peace and may the God of Israel grant the petition you have*

asked of Him... So the woman went her way and ate, and her face was no longer sad" (compare 1 Samuel 1:18 with Romans 10:17).
Like Habakkuk, Hannah's questions brought her a God-sized answer that put a smile on her face. God had a bigger purpose in his mind than her simply having a child. God was going to make her the mother of the great prophet Samuel who would speak God's word to the whole nation of Israel and anoint her first king. No wonder she waited in faith so long and prayed so hard.

Your questions will do the same. They will lead you to God. All you need to do is wait for his answers because such waiting is trusting. The Almighty is the one you are in a covenant relation-ship with. All smaller issues of life are meant to lead you to him who sits on the throne of the universe and to his good purpos-es for you. God is much bigger and better than you think, and his ways are always bigger and better. His heart is bigger. His thoughts are bigger. His plan is bigger. All that God is, and all that God does is bigger and better than your best.

I saw God's greatness many times during my twenty-two years in Zimbabwe. I wrote God's Sovereignty during the long political and economic crisis in the country. Time and again I saw God use manmade trouble to bring people to himself. When I first went to Zimbabwe, approximately five percent of her people attended church on Sunday. Today, well over half the population does. It is true that people often seek God and his answers when they face hard times and have nowhere else to look. Habakkuk did!

HABAKKUK
ASKING GOD WHY

- Asking God why is not contrary to a person's faith, but rather a potent act of faith and pathway to a deeper faith in God.
- Asking God why is the best defense against the unbelief of atheism and the doubt of agnostism.
- Asking God why flows out a belief that, through Christ, God is actively involved in your life and world–not a mere spectator, as theists hold.
- Asking God why often leads to additional questions to arrive at a more robust faith as you seek to understand what God is doing and how he plans to do it.
- Asking God why recognizes that God's ways are bigger and better than what you imagine.
- Asking God why will take you beyond what you see in your circumstances as well as what you currently know about God.
- Asking God why considers God's holy justice and tender mercies in conjunction with his sovereign attributes of being all-knowing, all-powerful, ever-present, and all-good.

HABAKKUK'S "WHY?" SUMMARIZED

You may face many troubles in this life, but whatever you face is permitted by a holy and merciful God for a good purpose. When life hurts and doesn't make sense, you can talk to God about it. When you face human and natural evil such as injustices and violence, a miscarriage, an accident, sickness, a broken relationship, unmet needs, shattered dreams, whatever may come. know that God is with you and for you and he will answer you! Remember, Habakkuk actually talked to God about his list of bad things. He didn't allow people or religious traditions to keep him from asking why. He had a relationship with God, not a mere set of beliefs, rules, or rituals. Do you have that kind of heart-to-heart communication with the Lord that empowers you to ask him why there is no food in the cupboard or peace on the home front? When your heart is heavy, do you fall on your knees and cry out to God? Do you voice the questions that plague your soul? Or are you afraid if you do, it will make matters worse?[17]

The book of Habakkuk answers personal loss in a new, dynamic way, which can propel you and me with greater purpose. The fresh answers Habakkuk received led him to a deeper faith, not based on circumstances. But if his questions were left unanswered, his difficult experiences could have left him confused.

Habakkuk learned that God uses whomever, whatever, whenever, and however he wills to accomplish his purposes. God's holy and merciful purposes are ever-redemptive. When he allows tests, it is to refine what is precious to him. When he disciplines, it is so that we are not condemned with the wayward world.

You and I encounter sin daily in our lives, but God knows how to deliver you.[18] That is the grand nature of our faith. You can trust that God is greater than what you are going through, and that he will turn the worse evil for the best good.

To understand this good fight of faith, you and I need to address another big question: *free will and the willful breaking of God's laws?* Questions related to sinful choices and suffering evil things land us at Jeremiah's door. The weeping prophet tells why there is suffering in this world. The straightforward answers he received will help you to better understand why people suffer.

CHAPTER THREE

JEREMIAH
SIN CROUCHING
AT THE DOOR

Because love grants free will that allows a world full
of individual and societal sins.

A woman at a park approached me with a clipboard. "Do you vote in Ohio?" Years ago, I was asked the same question outside a library for a petition on gambling that eventually became legal in my home state. "What's it for?" I asked. She pointed to large words on a clipboard, Reproductive Rights. "You aim to make abortions legal." "Yes!" she replied. I looked in her eyes, "Some believe abortion is murder, and if God feels that way, will he not hold me accountable if I sign this?" She walked away. 'Of all things,' I thought, 'on Mother's Day soliciting for a woman's right to kill her baby.' Many justify abortion. It's an accepted evil today, but the practice of murdering babies to secure some kind of future prosperity is ancient.[19]

Human Nature Hasn't Changed

The prophet Jeremiah, a contemporary of Habakkuk, confronted the people of Judah because in addition to all their other sins, *"They even sacrificed their sons and their daughters to demons, and shed innocent blood, the blood of their sons and daughters, whom they sacrificed to the idols of Canaan; and the land was polluted with blood."* (Psalm 106:37-38; Jeremiah 32:35).

You saw Habakkuk cry out against such sins and ask God why he didn't do anything about it. God answered him that the Babylonians would soon punish Judah. Remember, the prophet thought that God's cure was worse than their disease. But it's easy to misdiagnosis the sin condition, to brush it aside or think lesser remedies will cure it. But sin is lethal.

Judgement was decreed by God and Jeremiah warned the inhabitants of Jerusalem to submit to the King of Babylon, because God would not deliver them from him. They refused, however, and made their judgement more severe by adding rebellion to their sin *(Jeremiah 27:13-17; 32:3;36:29)*.

A few years later, Jeremiah saw the terrible consequences of Juda's rebellion when Habakkuk's prophecy was fulfilled. Jerusalem was laid waste, and Judah went to Babylon in cruel bondage. God had warned them and gave them time to repent, but when an individual or society allows too much wickedness for too long, God is obliged to bring judgement. Noah's flood and God raining fire down on Sodom and Gomorrah are examples.

The American Civil War is also an example of God's judgement. Those who lived then understood that. President Lincoln said, "Yet, if God wills that it (the war) continue until all the wealth piled by the bondsman's two hundred and fifty years of unrequited toil shall be sunk and until every drop of blood drawn with the lash shall be paid by another drawn with the sword as was said three thousand years ago so still it must be said 'the judgments of the Lord are true and righteous altogether.'"[20]

Before we ask God about how he deals with sin, he asks you and I a question: Why do you tolerate evil? Why not confront it? Why *"strain out a gnat and swallow a camel?" (Matthew 23:24).*

To restrain sin, God first sensitizes you to sin in your own heart. He gave Israel the Law to show them their willfulness. He gave you a conscience. He also uses people to admonish you. Before God judged Judah, he used Jeremiah to preach to his countrymen: *"The heart is deceitful above all things, and desperately wicked; who can know it?" (Jeremiah 17:9).*

Sin Answers Why People Suffer

Jeremiah's contemporaries made his life extremely difficult. Speaking truth on God's behalf to wayward hearts is always fraught with difficulties. Jeremiah's preaching and the persecution it provoked led to questions. He uses the word why thirty-seven times, about the same number of times as the word sin.

Jeremiah learned that sin was often the answer to the question of why there is suffering. He also learned that love meant both confronting Judah for their sinful lives and suffering at their hands. Jeremiah's questions and the answers God gave him will help you understand the sticky issues of your own life in society that is bent toward sin.

Let's look more deeply at what Jeremiah has to say about why Israel was plundered by the Babylonians: "*'Is Israel a servant? ... Why is he plundered? ... Have you not brought this on yourself, in that you have forsaken the Lord your God when He led you in the way?... Why will you plead with Me? You all have transgressed against Me,' says the Lord.*" (Jeremiah 2:14,17,29).

God had told Abraham he would spare Sodom and Gomorrah if he could find five righteous people there. He tells Jeremiah to look up and down the street of Jerusalem as the Lord would spare the whole city if could find anyone who seeks the truth. But they stole, murdered, committed adultery, swore falsely, burned incense to Baal, and walk after other gods (*Jeremiah 7:9*).

So God asked, *"How shall I pardon you for this? Your children have forsaken Me and sworn by those that are not gods. When I had fed them to the full, then they committed adultery and assembled themselves by troops in the harlots' houses...And it will be when you say, 'Why does the Lord our God do all these things to you?' then you shall answer them, 'Just as you have forsaken Me and served foreign gods in your land, so you shall serve aliens in a land that is not yours.'"* (Jeremiah 5:7, 19).

God warned Judah repeatedly, but they refused to listen and stiffened their necks like iron. Therefore, God send the sword, the famine, and the pestilence among them, till they were consumed from the land that he gave to them (*Jeremiah 24:10*). It is hard to suffer because you sinned or someone elsed sinned against you, but the prophet is clear that sin brings suffering.

"'Shall I not punish them for these things?' says the Lord. 'Shall I not avenge Myself on such a nation as this?'... Who is the wise man who may understand this? ... Why does the land perish and burn up like a wilderness, so that no one can pass through? And the Lord said, 'Because they have forsaken My law which I set before them, and have not obeyed My voice, nor walked according to it, but they have walked according to the dictates of their own hearts and after the Baals, which their fathers taught them.'" (Jeremiah 9:9,12-14).

Israel had a long history of idolatry in Egypt, in the wilderness, and in the Promised Land. God warned them as early as Moses that he would take back the land if they practiced idolatry *(Deuteronomy 4:26-31)*. It wouldn't matter how big a temple they had built or elaborate their feasts.[21]

It was no idle threat. Israel's captivity followed many lessons that their sins brought defeat and suffering at the hands of their enemies.[22] God drove that point home when they first entered the Promised Land. After the victory at Jericho, Israel was beaten at Ai by a weak, small army. *"So Joshua cried out, 'Alas, Lord God, why?'"* (Joshua 7:7-13). It was because of the sin of one man, Achan, who stole the accursed things *(Joshua 2:1-7:1)*.

Later, in the book of Judges, Gideon had the same question. *"O my lord, if the Lord is with us, why then has all this happened?"* (Judges 6:13). Sin again was the answer, and Israel tried half measures to obtain God's promises; they carried symbols of his presence, the Ark of the Covenant, and said loud prayers, even fasted. *"'Why have we fasted,' they say, 'and You have not seen? Why have we afflicted our souls, and You take no notice?'"* Because *"You fast for strife and debate, and to strike with the fist of wickedness.'"* (Isaiah 58:3-4; Jeremiah 14:12). When they returned to the land, God said, *"'You looked for much, but indeed it came to little; and when you brought it home, I blew it away. Why?' says the Lord of hosts. 'Because of My house that is in ruins, while every one of you runs to his own house.'"* (Haggai 1:9).

God did everything he could reasonably do to sensitize his people to restrain their sinful nature. Often, he called them to repent of their own ways. Often, they refused. So, he allowed them to experience the consequences of following their evil desires.

After their sins caught up with them, he wanted them to understand why they suffered. Repeatedly, he stated the reason: *"And it shall be, when you show this people all these words, and they say to you, 'Why has the Lord pronounced all this great disaster against us? Or what is our iniquity? Or what is our sin that we have committed against the Lord our God?' then you shall say to them, 'Because your fathers have forsaken Me,' says the Lord...And you have done worse than your fathers, for behold, each one follows the dictates of his own evil heart, so that no one listens to Me. ... Why do you cry about your affliction? ... Because of the multitude of your iniquities, Because your sins have increased, I have done these things to you."* (Jeremiah 16:10 -12; 30:15).

God also wanted the surrounding nations, who were not his people, to know the reason why Jerusalem was destroyed: *"And many nations will pass by this city; and everyone will say to his neighbor, 'Why has the Lord done so to this great city?' Then they will answer, 'Because they have forsaken the covenant of the Lord their God, and worshiped other gods and served them.'"* (Jeremiah 22:8-9).

Israel lost their blessed way of life, their days of rest, their joyful festivals, their Holy City, their temple, their kingdom, their long line of reigning descendants on David's throne. This was not because the Lord could not deliver them. Jeremiah makes it crystal clear it was because of sin and altogether avoidable. Self-induced suffering is truly the most tragic suffering of all. So, Jeremiah like Habakkuk, who foresaw the judgement coming, could not contain his emotions when this great tragedy came.

"O the Hope of Israel, his Savior in time of trouble, Why should You be like a stranger in the land, And like a traveler who turns aside to tarry

*for a night? Why should You be like a man astonished, like a mighty one
who cannot save? Yet You, O Lord, are in our midst, And we are called by
Your name; Do not leave us!"* (Jeremiah 14:8-9).

Despite Jeremiah's most tender and moving appeal, God tells him
that even if Moses and Samuel stood together interceding for
Judah, his mind would not be favorable to them *(Jeremiah 14:19)*.
Judah brought on their suffering. They only had themselves to
blame. *"'If you say in your heart, 'Why have these things come upon
me?' For the greatness of your iniquity your skirts have been uncovered,
your heels made bare.'"* (Jeremiah 13:22).

In lamenting Judah's suffering, Jeremiah states a most important truth that you and I need to continually affirm lest we get
the wrong idea about God, sin, and suffering: God does not afflict
willingly for his heart longs to show compassion. In Lamenta-
tions, Jeremiah writes, *"Though He causes grief, Yet He will show
compassion according to the multitude of His mercies. For He does not
afflict willingly, nor grieve the children of men.... Why should a living
man complain, a man for the punishment of his sins?"* (3:32-33,39).

Seeing into God's Heart

God causes grief, but he longs to show compassion, and the grief
he does cause, he does not cause willingly. The Hebrew word for
"willingly" is from the heart. God is long suffering, not willing
that any should perish *(2 Peter 3:9)*. He waited years in the days of
Noah till his righteous judgements overtook his tender mercies.
It is essential that we understand God's heart is rich in mercy.
He is the Father of mercies. He always rejoices in showing mercy
(James 2:13). Mercy triumphing over judgement is in keeping with
his most inner self, the deepest recesses of heart. God's heart is
seen in the face of Jesus when he hangs on the cross, breathing
his last breth while he forgives those who have murdered him.

When Moses asked to see God's glory, God revealed his heart, emphatically stating, *"Merciful and gracious, long suffering, and abounding in goodness and truth, keeping mercy for thousands, forgiving iniquity and transgression and sin, by no means clearing the guilty."* (Exodus 34:6-7).

This is God's consistent self-disclosure of his nature. His heart was tenderly expressed by the prophet Hosea: *"'When Israel was a child, I loved him, and out of Egypt I called My son.... I taught Ephraim to walk, taking them by their arms; But they did not know that I healed them. I drew them with gentle cords, with bands of love, and I was to them as those who take the yoke from their neck. I stooped and fed them.... How can I give you up, Ephraim? How can I hand you over.... My heart churns within Me; My sympathy is stirred'"* (Hosea 11:1-9).

Israel had sinned and deserved punishment, but there is a tension between God's mercy and justice, churning within. A loving parent knows this tension. God is a loving Father personified. He calls Israel, *"My dear son...My darling child....My heart yearns for him"* (Jeremiah 31:20).

The word heart here refers to the insides of a person, the guts, an image of the innermost recesses where a person's feelings reside. The word yearns is from a root word that means restless in that his emotions-affections are stirred.

There is a reluctance in God to send affliction. Something in his heart is against it. Even, when he does allow affliction, his heart is to restore. He takes no pleasure in the death of a sinner (Ezekiel 18:23). Whereas, when He shows mercy, he does it with all his heart, his complete disposition. So, God testifies through Jeremiah that when in his mercy he restores Israel he does it with rejoicing *"with all my heart, and all my soul"* (Jeremiah 32:41).

Imagine God restoring what you loss with all his heart and soul!

Restoration Delights the Heart

Our house in Africa was an old, dilapidated farmhouse on a beautiful two-acre lot. It took my wife and I years to turn it into a comfortable home as our family grew from two to four children. We did two new additions and several renovations. In My African Dream, Pat narrates the restoration. During the COVID lockdown, many housebound viewers watched YouTubes on restorations of French Chateaus. Patrice Besse said, "Owning a chateau is a 'way of life' and that many buyers care less about the return on their investment, and more about the emotional journey of restoring an old property and the dream of living in one."[23]

To restore is to delight. Before the Father could restore us from the ruins of sin and live inside us, his holy justice had to be fully satisfied. So, he sent his beloved son from his bosom to hang on a Roman cross. There Jesus poured out his life-giving blood in exchange for ours; thus, divine justice is served, and mercy shown. But the clincher, which gets to me emotionally, is that God himself weeps over our sins and the ruin it brings. Not only that but he himself suffers together with us the consequences of our rebellion to restore us to himself.

God's Heart and Jesus' Suffering

Like the law of gravity, "the law of sin and death" is found throughout the Bible. *"The soul who sins shall die" (Romans 8:2; Ezekiel 18:20).* But that does not mean that the Law Giver is aloof and detached from those who suffer the consequences of their sins. The opposite is true.

God himself also bares our suffering: *"Surely He has borne our griefs and carried our sorrows; Yet we esteemed Him stricken, smitten by God, and afflicted. But He was wounded for our transgressions, He was bruised for our iniquities; The chastisement for our peace was upon Him, and by His stripes we are healed. All we, like sheep have gone astray; We have turned, everyone, to his own way; And the Lord has laid on Him the iniquity of us all....*

In all their affliction, He was afflicted, and the Angel of His Presence saved them; In His love and in His pity ,He redeemed them; And He bore them and carried them All the days of old." (Isaiah 53:4-6; 63:9).

Jesus reveals God's glorious heart. He puts flesh and blood on the person of God, showing you what God is really like. Jesus is the express image of the invisible God. He is one with the Father. To see Jesus is to see the Father. When we see Jesus in the gospels moved with compassion, we see God's heart. God is the friend of sinners. He feels their weakness. He weeps with them and for them. He carries their diseases. He raises their dead. He says of his inner self, *"I am meek and lowly in heart" (Matthew 11:29).*

The series *The Chosen* is propular because it depicts a Jesus that is loving and caring. A Savior who wants you to offload your heavy burdens and give your soul rest. He sympathizes with all your struggles. He knows what it is like to be tempted, to feel weak, to experience all that we experience.

My mom lived to be ninety-seven. She was a very strong individual, Italian stock. They don't build them like the use "to make 'em." But as she grew old, she grew weak and her memory failed. She could read the same birthday card for an hour and smile repeatedly. I always loved my mom, but in her weakness, I love her more than in her strength. Isn't it also true that God wins your heart through his suffering in weakness on Mount Calvery? It is there you are won by grace rather than on Mount Sinai, the place where the law was given with all its powerful manifestations. It is there that God chooses to remember our sins no more.

Christ's passion and death helps you and I answer another big why. Why should Jeremiah suffer? The prophet hadn't sinned like his countrymen. He hadn't participated in their rebellion. He did the right thing, served God, and called his countrymen to repent. "Why?"

Lord, Why Me?

Love for sinners brought on his suffering. For love sakes the Messiah suffered. When you love someone, you willingly and patiently endure just about anything. You put your own needs second to the one you love. You even lay down your own life. But love is proved by what you do, not by what you say.

Jeremiah loved God and his neighbors from his youth. He was called by God's name. God's word was to him the joy and rejoicing of his heart. He never sat in the assembly of the mockers. He sat alone because God's hand was on him. God filled him with indignation over Judah's sin. He didn't just preach a message. He felt it deeply (Jeremiah 15:16-17).

"For the hurt of the daughter of my people I am hurt. I am mourning; Astonishment has taken hold of me. Is there no balm in Gilead, Is there no physician there? Why then is there no recovery For the health of the daughter of my people?" (Jeremiah 8:21-22).

Jeremiah had hoped his message would bring repentance, but it only brought more rebellion and persecution from those he loved. So, Jeremiah asked God plainly why he should experience such grief and pain. *"Why is my pain perpetual and my wound incurable, which refuses to be healed? Will You surely be to me like an unreliable stream, as waters that fail?" (Jeremiah 15:18).*

God explained to Jeremiah the reason for his pain. *"You shall be as My mouth" (Jeremiah 15:19).* To be God's mouthpiece, to speak his message right, as God would have it spoken, you need to experience it. As the saying goes, "The man is the Message." Jeremiah is thus called "the Weeping Prophet" for God weeps through Jeremiah. He grieved over the sins of his people. His grief was God grieving in him. It flowed out of his intimate relationship with God. Of all the prophets, Jeremiah thus comes across as entirely human, which is what God intended. For God himself would fully manifest himself as a human in the person of Jesus. Yes, God's truth and love find their fullest expression in Christ dying our death. We see in the Bible that the question of why is answered by a love that grants free-will, and by a love that can be returned or rejected, and by a love willing to suffer for the beloved.

PRINCIPLES FROM

JEREMIAH
ASKING GOD WHY

- Asking God why accepts that sin is an initial part of the answer to why there is suffering, and why people suffer many things.
- Asking God why is useful since God wants you to understand why you suffer, whether you suffer because of sins you committed or someone else committed.
- Asking God why enables you to understand the dynamics of love freely given and possibly rejected.
- Asking God why opens you to know God's heart of grief and sorrow over sin.
- Asking God why recognizes that you suffer for love's sake, and that God allows suffering to prove the depth of your love for him and others.

JEREMIAHS' "WHY?" SUMMARIZED

Like people in Jeremiah's day, the Christians at Corinth wondered why many were sick and dead. The apostle Paul didn't mix his words: "For this reason many are weak and sick among you, and many sleep. For if we would judge ourselves, we would not be judged. But when we are judged, we are chastened by the Lord, that we may not be condemned with the world." (1 Corinthians 11:30-33).

Jeremiah teaches us that the suffering we see is often the result of someone's sinful choices; it's the reason many hurtful things happen, why destruction fills the news.

God said to his prophet, "Call to Me, and I will answer you, and show you great and mighty things, which you do not know" (Jeremiah 33:2-3). The things God shows his people may be amazingly beneficial, like a land flowing with milk and honey, or terribly catastrophic like Babylon's violent siege of the Holy City. Yet, when you trust in God like Habakkuk learned to trust, you will bear the bad, while you rejoice in the truth of God's goodness. You'll ever believe and hope because, like Moses you've been to the mountaintop and seen his glory (1 Corinthians 13:4-8).

You may have personally wondered, Why didn't things work out the way I thought they should? Why did God allow that to happen to me? Why am I in such pain? Did I miss it somewhere? Is God punishing me?

We typically gravitate to Jeremiah's answer that sin is the reason. The dynamics and complexities of free will, sin, and the world you live in, however, are not the only answers to suffering. They provide partial answers to the questions of "why?"

Another essential element in the equation of "why" the suffering must be explored in light of the full counsel of God's word. That element brings us to the existence of supernatural evil and a man named, Job. Sin as the complete answer to suffering is far from the whole story as Job and his friends found out.

You and I do well to consider carefully this crucial component.

CHAPTER FOUR

JOB
THE ACCUSER
IN THE UNSEEN
REALM

Because of mighty, evil spirits that tempt, test, and wreak havoc,
and in their aftermath, tell lies that God is punishing you
or this would not have happened.

Meet the kind of man you would want as a father, brother, friend. He's honest, humble, patient, kind, wise, generous, fair, and compassionate. He's a man of deep faith. He loves God and his family. He cares for his workers. He's free of lust and greed. He provides for widows, orphans, the disabled, and strangers in need. He advances goodwill and fairness in the community so that the town elders seek out his counsel when making decisions.

Now that's a glimpse into the character of this man named Job. God called him *"upright."* Said he was *"blameless."* He *"reverences God and avoids evil." (Job 1:1-8).* The man stood out in Satan's domain among the multitudes on earth. He was the real deal. And you'll not meet a better mortal. Then he lost everything: his children, his wealth, his health. No wonder we find the word *why* twenty-two times in Job.

Job's friends heard the news of his demise and arrived to console him. For seven days, they didn't say a word because his loss was so great and his pain so deep. They were wise to say nothing. The tears they shed spoke louder than words. They provided Job with the comfort of their presence. But then, the inevitable question of why starts flying around.

Why Do the Righteous Suffer

After a two-chapter prologue set the stage of Job's outstanding character and his intense suffering, why appears seven times in chapter three. Why is Job suffering? It's the elephant in the room. It's an obvious question when you believe in a sovereign God, and you suffer. What did I do wrong?

Job raises the question obliquely as he considers his horrific loss: *"Why did I not die at birth? Why did I not perish when I came from the womb? Why did the knees receive me? Or why the breasts, that I should nurse? For now, I would have lain still and been quiet" (Job 3:11-13).*

Job doesn't curse God as his wife suggested, and as Satan alleged Job would do if God removed all his blessings. But Job did curse the day of his birth. He also raised age-old questions like *"Why is light given to him who is in misery, And life to the bitter of soul, Why is light given to a man whose way is hidden, and whom God has hedged in?" (Job 3:20,23).*

The Standard Answer

Such questions lead people of faith to speak about God, and Job's God-fearing friends could no longer keep quiet. They felt compelled to voice what they knew. But what they knew was not the whole story. Worse still, what they knew did not apply to Job. They possessed the long-standing doctrine that sin is ever the answer to the question, "Why?" You suffer because you sinned. The law of sowing and reaping was ingrained in them. What goes around comes around!

"Then Eliphaz the Temanite answered and said... 'Remember now, whoever perished being innocent? Or where were the upright ever cut off? Even as I have seen, Those who plow iniquity and sow trouble reap the same. By the blast of God they perish, and by the breath of His anger they are consumed'" (Job 4:1,7-9).

Among the godly, the doctrine of sin and suffering was rock solid. Man chooses to sin and suffers the consequences. Sin includes doing anything that is not right or failing to do something that is good, or somehow speaking or acting in a way that displays distrust or disloyalty toward God. And sin brings suffering. That answer has always been central to answering the question of why people suffer. Sin is a broad way and most everyone walks in it!

But did Job suffer because he sinned? Job's questions were a call for comfort, but his questions provoked his friends to reckon,

"You must've missed it!" They added insult to injury, and Job's suffering entered a realm of soul trauma. To conclude that God was judging him pushed Job near the edge of despair. To his credit, Job asked his friends, *"Teach me, and I will hold my tongue; Cause me to understand wherein I have erred"* (Job 6:24).

"Then Bildad the Shuhite answered and said: 'How long will you speak these things, And the words of your mouth be like a strong wind? Does God subvert judgment? Or does the Almighty pervert justice? If your sons have sinned against Him, He has cast them away for their transgression. If you would earnestly seek God And make your supplication to the Almighty, If you were pure and upright, Surely now He would awake for you, And prosper your rightful dwelling place. Though your beginning was small, Yet your latter end would increase abundantly.'" (Job 8:1-7).

Bildad conceded that maybe it wasn't you, Job, who sinned. But if it was not you, it must've been your kids. After all, they were the ones who died. Bildad maintained that the simple, straight equation remains true: *You do good, and God keeps you from harm. When you suffer, it is because you missed it somewhere.* His friends, however, continued to misinterpret what happened to him because they started with this wrong premise.

In the ancient world and in some religious circles today, God is like a vending machine. You put this in, and you get that out. It works–every time. Fallen humanity tries to control things, even the divine. But as Habakkuk discovered, God calls the shots, and trusting him is not based on what you see, but based on his sovereignty and character. Furthermore, the Most High is not cohered by what you do for his ways are absolutely perfect.

Questions Not Allowed

Bildad was concerned that Job questioned God's justice, which added to Bildad's premise that sin was the root cause.[24] If Job ever held to that doctrine, he didn't believe it any longer. And he let his friends know he was no longer buying it. His refusal to acquiesce provoked a redoubling of their efforts to shut him up, which went on forty chapters in the Book of Job.

Why did they believe that sin was always the answer? Because it was not only straightforward, but it was also often true. It's hard to tell when sin doesn't apply to suffering since all have sinned. It made for wise living. It provided a sense of security too. Life was too unsure without it. And people feared if the formula wasn't true, everyone would be in trouble as the same suffering could happen to them just as easily. *"You see terror and are afraid"* Job answered his friends. *(Job 6:21).* But mainly Job's friends held to this doctrine because it God off the hook. It was part of the package deal for good people. it comes with the turf: keep the rules, perform the rituals, speak the right words, and that includes defending the Almighty.

Whose to Blame

Centuries later, the sin equals suffering doctrine is still around. The Pharisees of Jesus' day had spread it far and wide.[25] In its starkest form, Jesus disciples asked him concerning a man born blind. *"Rabbi, who sinned, this man or his parents, that he was born blind?"* (John 9:2). The Lord's answer was a rebuttal of this simplistic formula.[26] *"Jesus answered, "Neither this man nor his parents sinned, but that the works of God should be revealed in him"* (John 9:3).

The sin answer didn't fit the blind man any more than it did Job. You would think that Jesus' answer would settle the matter, but still today, many hold to this basic answer as to why people suffer. It remains the gold standard answer to all the evil and suffering we see in this world. But Job teaches that the sin answer is not the only answer nor is it the whole answer.

Let's belabor the point by looking closely at the book's prologue, since I have heard word of faith teachers arguing that Job opened the door to his suffering by what he said and did, by acts of fear that showed a lack of faith.[27] They claim his sacrifices for his children were done out of fear, which opened the door to the Devil: *"For the thing I greatly feared has come upon me, and what I dreaded has happened to me" (Job 3:25).*

God himself, however, testified before the host of heaven that the cause of Job's suffering was not his sin: *"There was a man in the land of Uz, whose name was Job; and that man was blameless and upright, and one who feared God and shunned evil...Then the Lord said to Satan, 'Have you considered My servant Job, that there is none like him on the earth, a blameless and upright man, one who fears God and shuns evil?' ... Then Job arose {after he lost his children and wealth}, tore his robe, and shaved his head; and he fell to the ground and worshiped... In all this Job did not sin nor charge God with wrong" (Job 1:1,8,20,22).*

These verses could not be clearer that Job's sin was not the cause of his suffering. He was blameless. God said so in the highest court of heaven. The man became a target for that reason: *"Then the Lord said to Satan, 'Have you considered My servant Job, that there is none like him on the earth, a blameless and upright man, one who fears God and shuns evil? And still he holds fast to his integrity, although you incited Me against him, to destroy him without cause.' ... Then his wife said to him, 'Do you still hold fast to your integrity? Curse God and die!' But he said to her, 'You speak as one of the foolish women speaks. Shall we indeed accept good from God, and shall we not accept adversity?' In all this, Job did not sin with his lips." (Job 2:9-10).*

Job's response confirmed his righteousness, but even if he had sinned, his sin would not be the whole story. For personal sin and the sins of others as the cause of our suffering doesn't take into account a main culprit in all suffering: Satan and his evil

Principles and Powers attack and afflict people to test them and at times punish them for their sins.

Enter the Accuser

Job introduces Satan as plainly as anywhere in the Bible as the Accuser of the Brethren who brings afflictions to tempt, test, and trouble mankind. In my book, The Cleansing of the Heavens, I go into great details on what the Bible teaches regarding Satan's modus of operandi as the Accuser of the Brethren. That work, like that of a prosecuting attorney, was unlike his work on earth of deceiving and tempting, afflicting and killing humans, for it was done in heaven and directed at God, the holy judge of all.

There are many examples of Satan activity in the Old Testament that show him as an unbound Strongman who moved between heaven and earth with jurisdiction among humans due to their sins and his early dominion.

Here is an example how the Accuser of the Brethren acted in the heavenly courtroom: *"So Satan answered the Lord and said, 'Does Job fear God for nothing?... You have blessed the work of his hands, and his possessions have increased in the land. But now, stretch out Your hand and touch all that he has, and he will surely curse You to Your face!' And the Lord said to Satan, 'Behold, all that he has is in your power; only do not lay a hand on his person.' So Satan went out from the presence of the Lord"* (Job 1:9-12).

Job lost his children in a worst-case scenario when his sons and daughters were eating and drinking wine in their oldest brother's house. Before that, he had lost all his property. Then he lost his health at Satan's hand, not God's hand: *"And the Lord said to Satan, 'Behold, he is in your hand, but spare his life.' So Satan went out from the presence of the Lord and struck Job with painful boils from the sole of his foot to the crown of his head. And he took for himself a potsherd with which to scrape himself while he sat in the midst of the ashes" (Job 2:6–7).*

Suffering for What's Right

Job like Jeremiah and Moses suffered because they served God. They were imperfect, fallen people, but their suffering was not because of sins they committed. No, they suffered because they did something right, not something wrong! Obedience to God brought on their suffering at the hand of their enemy, and their supernatural enemy, Satan, also often employed natural enemies like the Sabeans against Job *(Job 1:15)*.

When they suffered, they asked God, "Why?" Because they realized everyone falls short of God's glorious standard; yet, they also knew that they were in right standing with God, based on his word, and the witness of their own conscience, which excused them from willful sins of rebellion.

Read how Job framed his why question for God: "*'What have I done to you, O Watcher of Men? Why have you set me as a target so that I am a burden to myself? Why then do You not pardon my transgression, And take away my iniquity? For now, I will lie down in the dust, and You will seek me diligently, but I will no longer be'"* (Job 7:20–21).

Exposing an Enemy in Heaven

Job found out that Satan was the source of his suffering. In the book that bears his name, he learned that God had granted the Devil permission to test him. But at the time, Job and his friends were unaware of what was happening in heaven, that lofty and vast realm of the spirit. They did not know that Satan accused Job of shallow, self-centered service of God and was permitted to test his accusation against Job for a greater redemptive purpose. Job's friends reverted to the only thing they knew.

Sin brings suffering and you must never question God (*Job 9:14; 10:15*). They knew there was no one who always does what is right and never sins. To them, Job's questions sounded impious. Therefore, they try to shut Job up without any understanding of this conflict in the unseen realm. But Job's questions are genuine, and as we are seeing, it is not wrong to ask God why when you suffer loss.

My grief journey, narrated in Blindsided, is driven by the "why" question.[28] In it, I discuss with my sons, Ethan's older brothers, who both studied theology, the question of why God permitted Ethan's death. We made a list of possible answers as I wondered: *Am I suffering like Job? Or did Ethan or I open the door to Satan?* I knew that God must have allowed my son to die for a good reason and purpose.

In asking why, I wasn't challenging God's sovereign right to do with Ethan and me whatever He willed, but I asked God to tell me his reason because I sought to understand his purpose and cooperate with his will.

"God doesn't have to tell me why," I admitted to his siblings, "but Jesus answered his followers' questions. He told Paul why he had a thorn in his flesh. He even told John who it was who would betray him." Because I had taught Job at college, I knew God had answered Job and I knew that Satan had a hand in my greatest loss. Because Job is part of the Bible's wisdom literature, it raises this vital question and other important questions.

Job raised another key contradiction to sin equals suffering. His objection to that formula was *"Why do the wicked live and become old, Yes, become mighty in power?"* (Job 21:7). Jeremiah asked it this way: *"Righteous are You, O Lord, when I plead with You; Yet let me talk with You about Your judgments. Why does the way of the wicked prosper? Why are those happy who deal so treacherously?"* (Jeremiah 12:1).

Is There a Doctor in the House

Jobs' friends had no real answers to his questions. Job called them miserable comforters and physicians of no value: *"Then Job answered and said... 'To him who is afflicted, kindness should be shown by his friend, even though he forsakes the fear of the Almighty. My brothers have dealt deceitfully like a brook, like the streams of the brooks that pass away.'"* (Job 6:1,14-15).

The analogy of a physician is instructive for those who care for hurting souls. A rule for doctors is "first do no harm to the patient." The Latin phrase, "primum non nocere" means that the potential benefits must outweigh the risks of harm since most treatments have possible adverse outcomes and medications have side efforts. The movie by the name, *First Do No Harm*, tells the story of doctors who only advise their patients of treatment options they favor.[29]

Doctors must be aware of their limitations in ability and knowledge. They should propose tests to determine the nature of the ailment, which is akin to soul doctors asking questions to ascertain the nature of one's affliction. A proper diagnosis is fundamental to proper treatment, whereas ignorance of the state of the patient opens the patient to further harm and injury. In other words, if the doctor has not rightly diagnosed your case, he is not likely to be successful in his treatment of it. A doctor must also exercise skill in the use of remedies like the drugs he prescribes, or he will poison his patients. He must not overestimate his capacity to heal, nor underestimate his capacity to cause harm.

The treatment Job experienced at the hands of his doctor friends was a hurtful 'one size fits all.' According to their standard practice of treatment they dispensed the sin is why you suffer medicine. God must be chastising Job for some secret sin (Job 9:29; 10:2; 13:24; 19:22).

PRINCIPLES FROM

JOB
ASKING GOD WHY

- Asking God why means you believe that God is sovereign and that his providence permeates all aspects of your life.
- Asking God why means that when you suffer, you will innately seek to understand the reason for your suffering.
- Asking God why means that although everyone has sinned, you learn that sin is not always the answer to suffering for some suffer because they are doing what is right.
- Asking God why means that it essential to acknowledge the multifaceted possibilities of why you suffer to properly address the reason and find an answer.
- Asking God why means you accept that you are involved in a great cosmic conflict with a supernatural Adversary who has a part in human afflictions.
- Asking God why means you understand God permits evil actions and the painful consequences for a greater redemptive purpose: the testing of faith and love, the formation of character, the evidence of his justice and mercy, the winning of others to faith, the defeat of evil by good, etcetera.
- Asking God why means that you ask out of a covenant relationship with God and a desire to cooperate with him.
- Asking God why means that God's answer will affect how you respond to suffering, knowing that the eternal outcome willfar surpass the temporary agony.
-

JOBS' "WHY?" SUMMARIZED

Job answered the question why the righteous suffer.[30] It provides a wise answers to that question unlike the folly of atheists who say, "Hey, Job, there's no One out there. The universe and you are chance events of evolution. Suffering is part of a cosmic CrapShoot."

However, when Job was overwhelmed by pain and sorrow, he continued to believe in God, the creator of all things, seer of all things, and hearer of his every cry for answers and help. He asked God why like Moses asked God why and not like the Israelites did in the wilderness. Job looked for real answers to his losses. He sought to cooperate with God's purposes.

Job's friends, like some religious people today, believe that asking God questions is a challenge to his authority. They believed that questions lead to unbelief. Job contended, however, that not asking God is what breeds unbelief and showed a lack of faith. Job's questions like those of Moses, Habakkuk, and Jeremiah led him to a deeper and fuller faith. His questions explicitly revealed the warfare dimension to faith, that we all struggle against a great, supernatural Adversary who seeks our harm.

In heaven, I will seek Job out to thank him for his integrity. But I will thank God even more for hearing Job's cry and recording his questions: *"Oh, that my words were written! Oh, that they were inscribed in a book! That they were engraved on a rock with an iron pen and lead, forever!" (Job 19:23-24).*

God used Job to teach us that it is alright to ask the Lord why you are suffering, to be honest with him about how you feel, to believe him for answers, because you know ultimately, he is in control, and that the Devil can only do what God permits, and

when God permits Satan to strike it is for a good reason.
Job is a good physician. He provides many instructions for
caregivers to the hurting. He calls us to ease pain by providing
comfort for the body and soul, to weep with those who weep, to
never tell the wounded how they should feel or what they should
or shouldn't say. We do not attempt to shut up their complaints,
nor do we offer cliches. We do not advise the sufferer against
asking God "why?" Nor do we deny that God gives answers. In
short, like a modest doctor, we don't play God.

Job teaches that suffering is not always because of sin. It may be
the opposite. The same tragic events affected Jeremiah and the
people of Judah, but the reasons for their suffering was as different as night and day. One suffered because he obeyed God. The
other because of disobedience.

My wife and I ministered in Zimbabwe during the peak of the
AIDS pandemic. We saw many families decimated. Often, an
unfaithful husband brought the HIV virus home to his wife, and
she died before him. We also saw many children born with the
disease die before their second birthday. We watched a graveyard
double in size over the span of a few years. It was awful. You
and I live in a sinful, broken world where sin is pervasive. That
is a huge part of the answer to suffering. But that answer is still
incomplete. It is not just human sin but supernatural evil powers
that harm people's lives.

More often than not, sin and suffering are not as black and white
as with Job and Jeremiah. It usually tends to be grey in most
people's lives: *"What did I bring on myself? What is a test? What is
from the Devil? What is chastisement from God? What is due to the sins
of others? What is for righteousness' sake?"* Those kinds of questions
bring us to the Book of Psalms and a man named David, who,
like all of us was a mix of the best and worse in human nature,
and who experienced the gamut of suffering and asked God

CHAPTER FIVE

DAVID
GOD'S OWN HEART FOR HIS CHILDREN

Because of an eternal, covenant relationship with God as Creator and Redeemer, which includes allowing us to suffer affliction for our own good and the benefit of others.

A story is told of a man who owned a donkey. The donkey was stubborn and would not let him ride it or do any kind of work. So, the man hired a donkey trainer. The trainer took out a stick and whacked the donkey twice, but the donkey hardly took notice. Then the trainer took out a sledgehammer and whacked him between the eyes. "You have killed my donkey!" the owner cried. "You have killed my donkey!" "No," the trainer said, "I just got your donkey's attention." And so, the training began...

You want someone's undivided attention these days with all the noise and distractions, you can't just talk. You must take away thier cellphones. Sometimes, God removes things from us to get our full attention for his detailed training.

There was a man named David. Although he didn't own a cell phone or a laptop, he understand what it meant to wait on God. Having his attention, the Lord trained him to be his warrior king: *"A Psalm of David. Blessed be the LORD my Rock, Who trains my hands for war, and my fingers for battle"* (Psalm 144:1).

King David learned the intricacies of successful warfare. He knew he had enemies and that his very life depended on God. In the Psalms, the practicalities of his prayers are recorded, including his heartfelt questions. God called David "a man after his own heart," which speaks volumes on how God feels about you and I being real with him *(1 Sam 13:14; Acts 13:22)*.

So, having previously established the validity, even the necessity, of voicing our "whys," let's now build on what we've learned from Moses, Habakkuk, Jeremiah, and Job as we hear David asking God "why" when life confronted him with troubles. Let's see how our prayers might benefit by adding this meaningful and perhaps missing dimension of communion with God. I know my prayers have been greatly enriched, because God loves it when we dialogue with him deeply on every facet of our life.

The sweet Psalmist of Israel not only asked God "why," he expected an answer. David is actually emphatic that God answered him, and he claims that God will answer you:

> "*May the Lord answer you in the day of trouble... Now I know that the Lord saves His anointed; He will answer him from His holy heaven with the saving strength of His right hand...May the King answer us when we call*" (Psalm 20:1,6,9).
>
> "*You have answered Me*" (Psalm 22:21).
>
> "*Hear, O LORD, when I cry with my voice! Have mercy also upon me and answer me*" (Psalm 27:7).
>
> "*You called in trouble, and I delivered you; I answered you in the secret place of thunder*" (Psalm 81:7 see John 12:29).
>
> "*In the day of my trouble I will call upon You, For You will answer me*" (Psalm 86:7).
>
> "*He shall call upon Me, and I will answer him*" (Psalm 91:15).
>
> "*Moses and Aaron were among His priests, And Samuel was among those who called upon His name; They called upon the LORD, and He answered them... You answered them, O LORD our God; You were to them God-Who-Forgives, Though You took vengeance on their deeds*" (Psalm 99:6,8).
>
> "*Incline Your ear to me; In the day that I call, answer me speedily*" (Psalm 102:2).
>
> "*I called on the LORD in distress; The LORD answered me and set me in a broad place*" (Psalm 118:5).
>
> "*I will praise You, For You have answered me*" (Psalm 118:21).
>
> "*I have declared my ways, and You answered me*" (Psalm 119:26).
>
> "*In the day when I cried out, You answered me, And made me bold with strength in my soul*" (Psalm 138:3).
>
> "*Hear my prayer, O LORD, Give ear to my supplications! In Your faithfulness answer me, and in Your righteousness... Answer me speedily, O LORD; My spirit fails! Do not hide Your face from me, Lest I be like those who go down into the pit*" (Psalm 143:1,7).

David's prayers like those before him were rooted in actual events in his life like when his son, Absalom, rebelled against him and when Nathan the prophet confronted him over his adultery with Bathsheba *(Psalm 51: 52; 55; 142)*. Even when the historical setting isn't specifically stated, we know the Psalms were written in the crucible of life. For example, the subscription of Psalm ten, attributed to David, says, "A Psalm of David when...." Many Psalms contain the word "when" and provide the backdrop in David's life *(Psalms 3-9; 11-32)*.

When life confronts you with obstacles, you can choose to pray. When you don't know where else to turn, you can turn to God. When you hurt, you can allow God to comfort you and encourage you. For when you go to God with your hurting heart, he always hears and answers.

What Can God Do When Life Hurts

When the Twin Towers fell on 9/11, prayer increased for a season; yet it did not bring any real change to America's spiritual life. Nor did the COVID pandemic in 2019.[31] Lasting change in an individual or society requires not only loss but real chang.

In the Psalms, we hear the cry of the afflicted. Because the Psalmist believed in God's rule over his life, he asked God why he was suffering. In answer to his question, you will see from the Psalms twelve reasons why all of God's children suffer.

REASON #1 You are afflicted because you commit sin.

We have looked at this reason for suffering in detail, and David's sin robed his soul of joy, and his body of health. He told God that by having mercy on him, other sinners would be changed: *"Have mercy upon me, O God...Blot out my transgressions. Wash me thoroughly from my iniquity and cleanse me from my sin. For I acknowledge my transgressions... Make me hear joy and gladness, that the bones You have broken may rejoice... Restore to me the joy of Your salvation. And uphold me by Your generous Spirit. Then I will teach transgressors Your ways, and sinners shall be converted to You*" (Psalm 51:1-3, 8-13).

"God, I turn from sin," David said. Like a child who bumps his head or burns his hand, we learn more from pain than pleasure. But if God prevented pain regardless of what we did, we would become the most reckless and self-centered people imaginable.

REASON #2 You are afflicted because you are opposed by a supernatural enemy who seeks to harm you.

Like you saw with Job, David also recognized that it was not always because of his own sin that he suffered evil: *"For look, they lie in wait for my life; The mighty gather against me, not for my transgression nor for my sin, O Lord. They run and prepare themselves through no fault of mine"* (Psalm 59:3-4).

REASON #3 You are afflicted to test the genuineness of your faith in God, especially when you see evil people prosper.

The Psalmist raised the question: Why do the wicked prosper? When you see evil people prosper, people who deny God, do wrong, and hurt others, it can be a stumbling block. Asaph, an author of several Psalms, admitted that it was so troublesome to him that it almost caused him to stumble. It helps to see the context to Asaph question and the answer God gave him.

"Truly God is good to Israel, to such as are pure in heart. But as for me, my feet had almost stumbled; my steps had nearly slipped. For I was envious of the boastful when I saw the prosperity of the wicked. For there are no pangs in their death, but their strength is firm. They are not in trouble as other men, nor are they plagued like other men. Therefore, pride serves as their necklace; violence covers them like a garment.

*Their eyes bulge with abundance; they have more than heart could wish.
They scoff and speak wickedly concerning oppression; they speak loftily
.... Behold, these are the ungodly, who are always at ease; they increase
in riches. Surely, I have cleansed my heart in vain, and washed my
hands in innocence. For all day long, I have been plagued and chastened
every morning" (Psalm 73:1-14).*

Asaph was honest about how he felt when he watched men who
proudly spoke against God live free from sickness and tragedy.
They lived a full life, died surrounded by loved ones, and were
mourned by family and friends. They had their lands named after
them. Asaph was tempted to envy them. He wondered why God
allowed the wicked to live what looked like abundant lives.

God answered Asaph while he was worshipping the Lord in his
temple. He may answer you in your prayer closet. *"Watch and
pray" (Matthew 26:41; Mark 14:38; Luke 21:34-36).* The answer God
gave Asaph was a bright light for him and us:

*"When I thought how to understand this, it was too painful for me—
until I went into the sanctuary of God; then I understood their end.
Surely You set them in slippery places; You cast them down to destruction. Oh, how they are brought to desolation, as in a moment! They are
utterly consumed with terrors. As a dream when one awakes, so, Lord,
when You awake, You shall despise their image. Thus, my heart was
grieved, and I was vexed in my mind. I was so foolish and ignorant; I
was like a beast before You. Nevertheless, I am continually with You;
You hold me by my right hand. You will guide me with Your counsel, and
afterward receive me to glory. For indeed, those who are far from You
shall perish; You have destroyed all those who desert You for harlotry.
But it is good for me to draw near to God; I have put my trust in the Lord
God, that I may declare all Your works." (Psalm 73:16-24,27-28).*

It's a slippery place when God does a person good all their lives,
shinning his sun on them and providing them with all they need,

but the good God does them, which should have lead them to repentance, instead has them treating God like useless garbage to be removed from their lives.

I can't think of a deicer place than this on the day of judgement! The kicker is they are completely oblivious to what awaits them: *"Your thoughts are very deep. A senseless man does not know, nor does a fool understand this. When the wicked spring up like grass, and when all the workers of iniquity flourish, it is that they may be destroyed forever...The Lord is upright; He is my rock, and there is no unrighteousness in Him" (Psalm 92:4-7,15).*

REASON #4 You are afflicted to keep you on the narrow path to life, far from the way of wicked, because without affliction your sin nature will cause you to wander away from God.

Wisdom says that chastising the wicked for sin increases their wickedness and adds to their guilt. But it has the opposite effect on the upright *(Proverbs 9:8-12)*. The Psalmist declares, *"Before I was afflicted I went astray, but now I keep Your word... It is good for me that I have been afflicted, that I may learn Your statutes... I know, O Lord, that Your judgments are right, and that in faithfulness You have afflicted me... Unless Your law had been my delight, I would then have perished in my affliction" (Psalm 119: 67, 71, 75, 92).*

The Father disciplined his own children, all of them, for he would not have them condemned along with hypocrites. If a person is not disciplined by God, he is not a child of God *(Hebrews 12:1-11)*.

REASON #5 You feel afflicted because you're made for better things and will never be satisfied with less than God's best.

At times, the Psalmist was unsure why he felt afflicted but his soul felt cast down. So, being a godly person, he wisely inquired as to why he felt that way, searching to uncover the reason: *"Why* are you cast down, O my soul? And why are you disquieted within me?"* (Psalm 42:5). His praying soul urgently appealed to God, for he knew God was ever his answer and that the enemy to his soul was the source of the oppression he felt. *"O my God, my soul is cast down within me. I will say to God my Rock, 'Why have You forgotten me? Why do I go mourning because of the oppression of the enemy?'"* (Psalm 42:6, 9-10).

David did what he knew to beat his discouragement. He prayed. He also acknowledged God's faithful covenant love: "The LORD will command His lovingkindness in the daytime, and in the night His song shall be with me—*'A prayer to the God of my life'"* (Psalm 42:8). He then remembered how God had helped him in the past: *"Therefore I will remember You from the land of the Jordan, and from the heights of Hermon, from the Hill Mizar"* (Psalm 42:5-7). He then claimed God's help and hoped in him: *"Why are you cast down, O my soul? And why are you disquieted within me? Hope in God; for I shall yet praise Him, the help of my countenance and my God"* (Psalm 42:9-11). David knew how to talk to God and his own soul.

REASON #6 You experience affliction because your human relationships are less than what your heart was made for, and others often disappoint you.

King Saul sought to take David's life, and David wrote several Psalms while fleeing from his father-in-law. David refused to raise his hand against Saul because Saul was king. But David did cry out to God against Saul's treachery. Psalm eighty-eight has an especially poignant tone: *"LORD, why do You cast off my soul? Why do You hide Your face from me?"* (Psalm 88:14-15). David spent several lonely years fleeing Saul as a refugee, and unlike Psalm forty-four and fifty-one this prayer did not end on a happy note: *"Loved one and friend You have put far from me, and my acquaintances into darkness"* (Psalm 88:18). David's soul was traumatized by the abusive treatment he recieved from Saul.

REASON #7 You suffer because your body has the sentence of death in it and with each passing day you're closer to death.

"God condemned sin in the flesh" (Romans 8:4) when Jesus died on the cross. Sin, we have seen, resulted in death. It drove man from Paradise and seperated man from God. It is the largest reason why there is suffering in this world. My sin, your sin, someone else's sin, everyone's sin, all the way back to Adam. But God did never willed for sin to keep us from spiritual life so he condemned sin in the body of man and not his spirit. He could thus promise to raise you and I to new life:

"Will You work wonders for the dead? Shall the dead arise and praise You? Selah! Shall Your lovingkindness be declared in the grave? Or Your faithfulness in the place of destruction? Shall Your wonders be known in the dark?" (Psalm 88:10-12).

The Psalmist asked questions every dying person asks: *Am I gone forever? Do I cease to exist?* He asked questions while living and dying. His questions served to bring him to God and to his word. Feelings of fear, discouragement, and sorrow serve that purpose. All that you experience in life is meant to bring you to God, to call on him, to trust him, to find his will, to live in a restored relationship with him, to glorify him for your own good.

REASON #8 You are afflicted to prove that you trust God will make right what is wrong in your life and in your world.

David's trust is held in direct contrast to how unbelievers react. In affliction. unbelievers strike out at others. David was acutely aware of the tyrannical nature of evildoers, and he relentlessly interceded for God's intervention, which included asking God "Why?" David was no doormat nor was he passive in the face of evil. He did not avenge himself, but he did powerfully appeal to God to act against human wickedness. Read these verses slowly:

"Why do You stand afar off, O LORD? Why do You hide in times of trouble? The wicked in his pride persecutes the poor... For the wicked boasts of his heart's desire; he blesses the greedy and renounces the Lord. The wicked in his proud countenance does not seek God; God is in none of his thoughts. His ways are always prospering; Your judgments are far above, out of his sight; as for all his enemies, he sneers at them. He has said in his heart, 'I shall not be moved; I shall never be in adversity.' His mouth is full of cursing and deceit and oppression; under his tongue is trouble and iniquity. He sits in the lurking places of the villages; in the secret places he murders the innocent; his eyes are secretly fixed on the helpless" (Psalm 10:1,3-8; 77:7-9; 85:4-8).

The Psalmist insisted that God's lack of intervention had caused the wicked to think that God didn't see what they were saying and doing, and for evil doers to reckon that if he did, he mustn't care, which led them to say, *"God has forgotten; He hides His face; He will never see... He will not require an account"* (Psalm 11-13).

David rightfully makes their actions a personal affront against Lord since they called God's character into question, while David quickly voices his trust in God: *"But You have seen, for You observe trouble and grief, to repay it by Your hand"* (Psalm 10:14).

David was assured as he prayed that God would hold the wicked accountable as well as deliver the poor and needy, the widow and fatherless, regardless of the way things looked. This is the answer Habakkuk and the prophets received when they observed evil doers in action. They trusted God, even when evil called into question God's existence and goodness.

David didn't just wait for a far off judgement day. He drove home God's responsibility to act: *"The helpless commits himself to You; You are the helper of the fatherless. Break the arm of the wicked and the evil man; seek out his wickedness until You find none"* (Psalm 10:14-15).

This is intercessory prayer at its best despite its imprecatory nature. But such prayers are nolonger prayed and many consider them un-Christian.

REASON #9 You are afflicted because you stand against evil.

If God doesn't act against evil doers, David pledges to stand against them, and he called others to help him: *"Who will rise up for me against the evildoers? Who will stand up for me against the workers of iniquity?" (Psalm 94:16).*

After the Psalmist presented his case, he praised God and again affirms his trust in what God will do to make it right: *"The LORD is King forever and ever... You have heard the desire of the humble; You will prepare their heart; You will cause Your ear to hear, To do justice to the fatherless and the oppressed, that the man of the earth may oppress no more." (Psalm 10:17-18).*

You might think that this standing up to evil does not apply to many people, but would it not include all the soldiers or police or ordiary people who have fought to stop the abuse of tyrants?

REASON #10 You are afflicted because of your zeal for God's Name and people, even if it means going against the world.

In Psalm seventy-four, the Sweet Psalmist of Israel prayed when Israel's enemies laid their land desolate, destroyed their city, and tore down their temple. He asked why and called on God to act: *"O God, why have You cast you off forever? Why does Your anger smoke against the sheep of Your pasture? O God, how long will the adversary reproach? Will the enemy blaspheme Your name forever? Do not forget the life of Your poor forever."*

He asked God to "respect the covenant" he made with them. He also appealed to the Lord's reputation among the nations:

"Remember this, that the enemy has reproached, O LORD, And that a foolish people has blasphemed Your name.... remember Your congregation, which You have purchased of old." "Why do You withdraw Your hand, even Your right hand? Take it out of Your bosom and destroy them" (Psalm 74:1-23; see also Psalm 80:1-19).

REASON #11 You are afflicted because you are part of a much larger story than you realize.

That story is centered in death and resurrection, in suffering before glory, pain before gain, thorns before thrones, going down before up, and affliction before comfort, humility before honor....

Psalm forty-four boldly claims that all this bad has happened to them, even though they were faithful to God and worshipped him alone. He argues that God had sold them for next to nothing. He compares them to sheep led to the slaughter. For God's sake, they were killed all day long. You have got to read this one for yourself. It reads like Job on a national level. And the implication is mind blowing. It can only be understood in the light of much bigger storys being told by Someone much bigger than you think:

"In God we boast all day long and praise Your name forever. Selah, But You have cast us off and put us to shame, and You do not go out with our armies. You make us turn back from the enemy, and those who hate you have taken spoil for themselves. You have given us up like sheep intended for food and have scattered us among the nations. You sell Your people for next to nothing and are not enriched by selling them. You make us a reproach to our neighbors, a scorn, and a derision to those all around you. You make us a byword among the nations, a shaking of the head among the peoples... All this has come upon us; but we have not forgotten You, nor have we dealt falsely with Your covenant. Our heart has not turned back, nor have our steps departed from Your way; but You have severely broken us in the place of jackals and covered us with the shadow of death." (Psalm 85:8-19).

What the Psalmist experienced seemed so contrary to God's covenant promises it begs for an answer as to why God had allowed all this happened to them:

"If we had forgotten the name of our God, or stretched out our hands to a foreign god, would not God search this out? For He knows the secrets of the heart. Yet for Your sake we are killed all day long; we are account- ed as sheep for the slaughter. Awake! Why do You sleep, O Lord? Arise! Do not cast us off forever. Why do You hide Your face, and forget our affliction and our oppression? For our soul is bowed down to the dust; our body clings to the ground. Arise for our help, and redeem us for Your mercies' sake" (Psalm 85:20-26).

The story includes their affliction because they are closely identi- fied with the One who the story is all about. It is His-story!

REASON #12 You are afflicted because it is a righteous thing with God to repay those who trouble you with trouble!

Before God gives you eternal glory and everlasting rest from trouble, and before he consumes the wicked, including Satan and all his demons, he allows them to afflict you for a short ssason.

It helps to know the above twelve answers to why people suffer *(2 Thessalonians 1:6-9; Hebrews 11:23ff)*. Why God allows the Evil one to strike those who are innocent and vulnerable, why he doesn't stop Satan in his tracks, why he puts up with his wick- edness, why he doesn't just throw him into the Lake of Fire?

Lest we fail to grasp these truth, there's a point worth stating: *when God throws Satan and his angels into the Lake of Fire, he will in his justice forever remove all that offends and causes sin.* That includes all who are unrepentant, which may include someone you love. And God is not willing that any should perish, he patiently waits until his last prodigal child comes home to him.

DAVID
ASKING GOD WHY

- Asking God why is a vital part of prayer and communication with God.
- Asking God why is birthed out life's experiences like suffering, facing injustices, and watching ungodly people prosper.
- Asking God why is part of intercessory prayer and appealing to God's honor.
- Asking God why keeps watch over the condition of your soul particularly when it is troubled and discouraged.
- Asking God why helps you avoid misinterpreting God's Word, especially when His covenant promises seem to fail.
- Asking God is taught in the law, in the prophets like Jeremiah, in wisdom literature like Job, in the writings like the Psalms of David.
- Asking God why is a means to peace and praise as we have seen in the Psalms.
- Asking God why proves itself again to be an expression of faith and love for God.

DAVIDS' "WHY?" SUMMARIZED

David's prayers to God are far more vulnerable than most human conversations, and they sound far less religious than most prayers you will hear in churches today. Some would have you believe that these types of prayers have no place in God's house, but they are wrong. God answered mightily the cry of Daivd's heart, and God has not changed.

The twelve reasons found in the Psalms as to why God allows suffering are not exhaustive, but they do bring you and I to the most provocative and consequential "WHY?" ever uttered!

That "Why, God?" is also in the Psalms of David, and Jesus chose to quote it from the cross before he breathed his last breaths: *"My God, My God, why have You forsaken Me? Why are You so far from helping Me, and from the words of My groaning?" (Psalm 22:1).*

The answer to that question cannot be overstated. As we will see in the final two chapters, the answer to why Jesus was forsaken on the cross encompasses the whole of the Christian life and your experience as a believer.

So, let's move to the New Testament and look at Jesus' question regarding his own suffering, and the answer he received. Then, after Jesus, you and I will conclude our deep dive into the why of suffering will Paul's suffering as an example of a believer.

If you have afflicted your soul by reading this far, bravo! Comfort is coming because Christ has come....

CHAPTER SIX

JESUS GOD'S SALVATION

Because God's only way to save us from our sins
required Jesus to suffer and die the death we deserved.

Children are curious. They ask questions. But then–they stop. It's not, as if in their teens, they have all the answers, despite their smart phones. But after years of learning what's 1+1 or how do you spell dog, they feel they should have answers. But you must never stop asking questions, whether you follow or lead.[32]

"Leaders today need to revisit an overlooked skill: asking questions.... By asking questions as a leader, you also communicate that questioning is important... leads to a culture of learning."[33]

Rabbis, Jewish religious leaders, recognized the power of questions, and Jesus, the wisest rabbi ever, posed real life questions to his followers.[34] In a storm, *"Why are you fearful?"* When they *worried about food, "Why do you reason among yourselves because you have brought no bread?"* (Matthew 8:26; 14:31:16:8). He questioned their reasons for fear and called them to a new perspective because entering and serving in his kingdom required faith and new paradigms *(Matthew 6:28-30; 7:38; 21:25; Mark 8:12-17; Luke 6:46; 24:38; John 7:19; 8:46)*.

Jesus encouraged their questions, and they asked him questions on everything from the types of sermons he preached, *"Why do You speak to them in parables?"* to what the scribes taught, *"Why then do the scribes say that Elijah must come first?"* to why their deliverance ministry failed, *"Why could we not cast it out?"* to *even how money should be spent, "Why was this fragrant oil wasted?* (Matthew 13:10; 17:10,19; 26:8,10).*

Amazingly, Jesus answered all their questions, from the day he called them to his Last Supper. *"Lord, why can I not follow You now? I will lay down my life for Your sake."* He even answered the vexing *question of who would betray him (John 13:21-26,37)*. Never once did he rebuke his disciples for asking questions. He used them as opportunities to teach and apply truth.

Jesus also answered his detractors' questions. *"Why do Your disciples transgress the tradition of the elders?"* (Matthew 15:2). *"Why then did Moses command to give a certificate of divorce?"* (Matthew 19:7). *"Look, why do they do what is not lawful on the Sabbath?"* (Mark 2:24). *"Why do You eat and drink with tax collectors and sinners?"* (Luke 5:30). He answered them all.

It astounds me how willingly Jesus answered the questions of friends and foes. He even answered questions that sought to trap him. *"'Shall we pay (taxes to Rome), or shall we not pay?'"* (Mark 12:15). The only question Jesus did not answer was when he was on trial.[35] *"Do You answer nothing?"* Again, the high priest asked him, *"Are You the Christ, the Son of the Blessed?"* Jesus answered openly, *"I am. And you will see the Son of Man sitting at the right hand of the Power and coming with the clouds of heaven."* Jesus' sincerity was contrasted to the hypocrisy of the religious leaders. *"Then the high priest tore his clothes and said, 'What further need do we have of witnesses? You have heard the blasphemy!'"* (Mark 14:60-64).

We have examined the questions that the Old Testament saints asked God. We've also seen how Jesus asked questions and answered them. We have, thus, prepared our hearts to consider the most profound question in the Bible. It is the question that Jesus alone could ask his Father while he died upon the cross. It reveals the depth of what he suffered to redeem us. But before we take that deep dive, let's ponder the background to it.

JESUS' WEIGHTY QUESTION FOR HIS FATHER

To understand Jesus' question, we must go with him to a garden named Gethsemane. In that quiet garden, his passion begins. There he began to be troubled and deeply distressed. There you see Jesus unlike anywhere else in the gospels. *"My soul is exceedingly sorrowful, even to death."* There you see him falling on his face on the ground, praying, *"If it were possible, the hour might* pass from Him. And He said, 'Abba, Father, all things are possible for You. Take this cup away from Me; nevertheless, not what I will, but what You will'" (Mark 14:32-36; Matthew 26:39).

Most Christians think that Jesus was asking his Father to spare him from physical death. But Jesus knew the prophetic Scriptures. "They pierced My hands and My feet; I can count all My bones" (Psalm 22:1, 16-17). On the cross, he quoted that Psalm. He openly told his followers he would die by crucifixion, and he rebuked Peter for contending against it (Mark 8:31-22).

Christ was the Lamb slain before the foundation of the world. This was part and parcel of what the Messiah would do. Jesus did not go back on what he knew and preached. He was not asking his Father to spare him from death, even death by crucifixion.

WHAT WAS JESUS ASKING HIS FATHER?

Beyond the physical descriptions of crucifixion in the Psalms, Isaiah foretold that the Messiah's soul would be offered up for sin. All our iniquities and transgressions, our sins and the chastisement of our peace would be placed on Jesus, our substitute. He would bear the curse our rebellion deserved (Isaiah 53:1-12). He knew these dreadful Scriptures, and they described more than bodily suffering.

"When You make His soul an offering for sin" (Isaiah 53:10).

Jesus' emotions "exceedingly sorrowful" and his praying prostrate "on his face" were in response to "this cup." Christ prayed that "the hour might pass from Him" as he taught his disciples to pray that they enter not into temptation. The intent of his prayer was to get through this most awful time. The content of his request was that "this cup might be removed."

Luke, the physician among the four gospel writers, researched everything related Christ's life and death. He noted that Jesus was sweating blood—a rare but well documented medical condition, when a person experiences unbearable anguish *(Luke 1:1-4; 22:44)*. As Jesus felt the weight of what was coming, it was so heavy that he experienced hematidrosis, and cried out three times that if God were willing to take *"this cup"* from him. Yet, if he must drink, not his will, but the Father's be done *(Luke 22:42)*.

WHAT WAS IN THIS CUP THAT JESUS SO GRAVELY PRAYED FOR IT TO BE REMOVED?

Bible scholars call it a cup of suffering, which it was, but the ingredients and the type of suffering this cup held, was far more than the torturous pain, inflicted by crucifixion, as painful as that was, and it contained more than the shameful ridicule, thrown at him by the gathered mob. For we know the martyrs, like Stephen, endured physical death and public ridicule with a peace that surpasses understanding, which comes from God's close, empowering presence. But that was not the case with Jesus. *"Why?"* What was in "this cup?"

In several places, the Bible speaks of *"this cup"* *(Psalm 11:6; 75:8; Isaiah 51:11, 22; Jeremiah 25:15)*. It was full of man's iniquities and infidelity to God. *"Cup full of abominations and the filthiness of her fornication"* *(Revelation 17:4; 18:24)*. All the evil choices of every person who ever lived, each act of violence, deception, immorality, corrupt speech, thievery, idolatry, covetousness – all the wickedness you could ever imagine since Adam.

It was, therefore, also a cup full of sorrow, horror, and desolation. The worse trauma the world, the flesh, and Satan could convey. Ezekiel calls it *"the cup of grief and sadness"* *(Ezekiel 23:33)*. [36] The Living Bible reads, *"You will feel like a drunkard beneath the awful blows of sorrow and distress."* The Amplified Bible says, *"You shall be filled with drunkenness and sorrow, with the cup of wasting astonishment and horror."*[37]

No wonder Jesus' soul was *"exceedingly sorrowful to the point of death."* It is a cup appointed for sinners to drink. *"For in the hand of the Lord there is a cup, and the wine is red; It is fully mixed, and He pours it out; Surely its dregs shall all the wicked of the earth drain and drink down"* (Psalm 75:8).

"This is the cup of ruination, of destruction" that will *"completely destroy you,"* *"a cup canyon-deep and ocean-wide. You'll be shunned and taunted as you drink from that cup, full to the brim. You'll be falling-down-drunk, and the tears will flow as you drink from that cup titanic with terror."*[38] *"The cup of dismay, astonishment, and desolation"*[39] (Psalm 11:6; 75:8; Isaiah 51:17; Jeremiah 25:15; 49:12).

"This cup" held God's enduring hatred and intense wrathful judgement against human evil. Because God is love, he is angry at all that degrades and destroys you. Sin is the moral sickness that disfigured your beauty and brought death to life he gave you. As a mother hates the polio that takes the life of her child, God hates sin. With his entire being, he cannot but destroy it.

The eschatological fulfillment of God's wrath against sin is in the Lake of Fire. Eternal judgement includes a cup that is drank: *"He himself shall also drink of the wine of the wrath of God, which is poured out full strength into the cup of His indignation. He shall be tormented with fire and brimstone in the presence of the holy angels and in the presence of the Lamb"* (Revelation 14:10; 16:9).

With his impending arrest, Christ knew what was coming his way: *"Jesus therefore, knowing all things that would come upon Him"* (John 18:4). *"This cup"* was near at hand, and Jesus began to catch whiffs of the repulsive stench of its contents. Imagine his emotional and volitional struggle as he anticipated drinking down the fierceness of God's wrath against sin. His heavy, sorrowful heart testified to the fact that he was acutely aware of what it would mean to imbibe the recompense of man's sin. That knowing prompted his profound trial in the garden.

So, Christ prayed that the ingredient of being cut off like a condemned sinner might be removed from that cup. For he had never known anything remotely associated to distance from God. It was totally contrary to his relationship to his Father.

Let's, therefore, ponder ten points as to why drinking "this cup" was so extremely difficult and yet so very necessary:

1st Consider how close Jesus was to his Father.

They were one. Jesus often spoke of their closeness. So close that *"No one knows the Son except the Father. Nor does anyone know the Father except the Son, and the one to whom the Son wills to reveal Him" (Matthew 11:27)*. You see that tenderness between Jesus and his Father an hour earlier, before his ordeal in Gethsemane. John records Christ's intimate prayer in the Upper room: *"They are Yours. And all Mine are Yours, and Yours are Mine...You loved Me before the foundation of the world... the love with which You loved Me (John 17:9-10, 20, 24, 26)*.

I spoke to a friend, a newspaper reporter, and asked him, "How's your relationship to God?" He replied in one word, "Distant!" It doesn't have to be that way. We were all distant to God but are *"brought near by the blood of Christ" (Ephesians 2:13)*. But for us to experience God's nearness Christ had to drink dreadful cup.

2nd Consider how contrary this cup was to Christ's nature.

To drink of such a cup was completely contrary to Christ's righteous soul. His just mind, his good will, his godly emotions, his pure heart, his untainted spirit were horror stricken. Imagine how all the evil acts of wicked people caused such a good person to cringe and cry out in trauma *(Job 15:16; Proverbs 4:17)*. He would soon know what the soul of a condemned sinner feels when *"his soul was made an offering for sin" (Isaiah 53:10)*. For he would not only bear human sin, but he would become human sin. *"For He made Him who knew no sin to be sin for us, that we might become the righteousness of God in Him (2 Corinthians 5:21)*.

3rd Consider Christ's steadfast experience with his Father.

To drink such a cup was completely opposite to Jesus' experience with his Father from all eternity. He dreaded that sense of separation from his Father's life and love, cast for the first time as it were from his Father's bosom into the bowels of hell. It was a dimension of suffering you and I will never know: *"The soul that sins it shall die" (Ezekiel 18:4,20; Hebrews 2:9, 5:7)*. *"But we see Jesus, who was made a little lower than the angels, for the suffering of death crowned with glory and honor, that He, by the grace of God, might taste death for everyone" (Hebrews 2:9)*.

4th Consider Jesus' love for you and his Father that willingly bore the curse of your sin.

Christ bore the curse of God's broken law as he hung on that tree *(Deuteronomy 21:23)*. *"Christ has redeemed us from the curse of the law, having become a curse for us (for it is written, "Cursed is everyone who hangs on a tree")" (Galatians 3:13)*. Yes, Jesus had to drink that terrible cup that we might freely drink of the cup of salvation. For you and me, and out of love for his Father, his soul drank, undiluted, the punishment our sins deserved to the last dreg. It is not that the Father stopped loving Jesus. *"Therefore, My Father loves Me, because I lay down My life that I may take it again" (John 10:17)*. But in drinking that foul mixture, Jesus' is unable to consciously experience that love. That love feels beyond reach.

5th Consider the answer the Father granted his Son's request.

The only answer the Father could grant in response to Jesus' plea was strengthen to go on. *"There appeared an angel unto him from heaven, strengthening him" (Luke22:43).* God can, therefore, also grant you strength to face whatever comes your way. For God willed for Jesus to drink the cup, because that was the only way God could take away man's sin. Jesus had to drink in the judgment our sin deserved *(John 1:29; Acts 4:12; Hebrews 10:14; Revelation 5:9).* So, it was, on the cross, Jesus also refused the cheap wine offered him to lesson his pain. For he drank a cup far more potent than physical death, a cup that held the mystery of iniquity and all uncleanness.

6th Consider the truth that Jesus had an option not to drink.

Jesus willed to do the Father's will not his own will. When Peter defended him with his sword, *"Jesus said, 'Put your sword in its place, for all who take the sword will perish by the sword. Or do you think that I cannot now pray to My Father, and He will provide Me with more than twelve legions of angels? How then could the Scriptures be fulfilled, that it must happen thus?'" (Matthew 26:52-54; John 18:11)* Jesus could've asked his righteous Father to send armies of angels to deliver him. But he did not. Instead. after he requested a less repulsive cup, he drank what the wicked should drink fully aware its dreadful, deadly ingredients.

7th Consider how grotesque and repulsive sin is to God.

When God created the world, holiness was the moral condition necessary to its health. Sin is a corruption. To preserve his creation, God must wipe away what would destroy his masterpiece. Every judgement in the history has thus been a holy act of preservation that God's creation might continue. A study of Scripture bears out that Satan attempted to cohabit with humans before the Flood and push humanity beyond redemption. You see, the Devil's evil activity to damn humans again in the lawlessness of the Last Days (*Genesis 6:1ff; Luke 17:26; 2 Thessalonians 2:5-12*).

How can mere mortals know what Jesus' soul endured? My dream served as a tiny insight. I was homeless in Katmandu. It is the filthiest city I've ever visited. I had no shoes, and my clothes were rags. I had to walk through sewage. When I tried to shower and pulled the cord to release what I thought would be water, a huge bucket of waste and urine was dumped on me. I was so filthy, street beggars looked at me in astonishment. *What has happened to me?* I could not get away from my own stench of rottenness and decay. It took every ounce of grace to stay. Although I wanted to escape in whatever way possible, I knew God had put me there to identify with and minister to the least. This was my mission field. So, I shook their hands and interceded for them like I had never prayed before. I woke up from the intensity of that experience with a twinge of what Jesus endured.

8th Consider that Jesus was delivered over to evil powers.

I'm sure the Evil One used everything and everyone at his disposal to stop Jesus' mission. At first, he offered Christ another way in keeping with his status as the Messiah. He would give Jesus all the kingdoms of the world if Christ would bow before him just once. Jesus refused. The Son of Man set his face like flint to go to Jerusalem. He would not turn away from the cross. So, the Devil gathered every evil force, and mustered all the might that wickedness possessed and hurled it all in Christ's face. Satan's full range of abuse, hatred, and rage, demons of blasphemy, religious legalism, pride, violence, lust, racism, enmity, and murder manifested themselves in increasingly vicious measures against Jesus. Satan used the religious leaders, the soldiers, and the people. The demons inside them surrounded Jesus like rabid dogs and angry bulls. They beset him as ravening and roaring lions. They shouted at him while he hung, agonizing on the cross. Their assaults became an anxious frenzy, chanting and tempting Jesus to come down from the cross. Had he done so, Satan would have succeeded in keeping humanity trapped in sin's bondage forever. Creation would have remained corrupt.

The Cleansing of the Heavens explains from Scripture how the death of Christ defeated Satan. It elaborates on redemption, the warfare dimension of Christ's death. You see, Satan corrupted his vast wisdom to establish a kingdom, built on sin and death. Temptations, seductions, and accusations became his modus operandi to hold humans in bondage. Before Jesus' death, Satan was a Strongman, and like a prosecuting attorney, he used God's holy law, broken by humans, to accuse and indict them of sin. He thus enacted the penalty of death on all who had ever lived for all had sinned. This dominion Satan exercised on humans was not from outside of them, but it was the working of the mystery of iniquity within their very souls, causing their spirits to be cut off from the life of God. Jesus' death and resurrection was the only act that could overthrew Satan's evil kingdom.

9th Consider that Jesus died such a death and rose to new life so that we could be recreated in him.

God created all things by Christ, and when his creation was defiled and devastated, his Word became flesh to redeem mankind and restore creation. Christ's redeemed creation through his death and God recreated it by his resurrection *(Colossians 1:16-17; Ephesians 2:1-3)*.

You may think I go too far in my assessment of what "this cup" contained, what it means that Jesus died our death. Do I make more out of it than was there? Is it possible to make too much of Christ vicarious, substitutionary death? The whole of the Bible leads to it and testifies that there was no other way.

The writer to the Hebrews refers to Jesus' prayers in Gethsemane, *"Who, in the days of His flesh, when He had offered up prayers and supplications, with vehement cries and tears to Him who was able to save Him from death... of whom we have much to say, and hard to explain, since you have become dull of hearing"* (Hebrews 5:7-9).

Note the writer to the Hebrews uses the plural *"things He suffered."* Jesus' suffering was more than physical. He wrote, Jesus' prayers were *"to him who was able to save him from death."* Yet, the Father did not deliver Jesus from physical death, although it says, *"he was heard."* So, what kind of death did the Father deliver him out of by his resurrection?

Adam died on the day he ate of that evil tree; he was cut off from the life of God, whereas his body only died many, many years later. The writer to the Hebrews concludes by saying, he has *"much to say, and hard to explain."* So, let us not be dull of hearing.

"Since the children have flesh and blood, he too shared in their humanity so that by his death he might break the power of him who holds the power of death-that is, the devil... because he suffered death, so that by the grace of God he might taste death for everyone" (Hebrews 2:9,14).

What was it like for Jesus to hang on that tree between heaven and earth, and to drink in and taste death? What does death taste like? What was it like for the Prince of Life to experience death?

Please bear with me, for I am done yet. There is one more huge point. No, I do not believe Christ died spiritually, or that he was tormented in hell. But I do believe more happened in his soul when he suffered and died upon the cross than we have articulated thus far. For drinking "this cup" revealed the reality behind the question Jesus asked his Father before his body died. It has to do with his sense of forsakeness.

10th Consider that Jesus experienced in his soul a sense of forsakeness, a sense of death, seperation from his Father, that enables you and I to be forever united to His Father.

"And at the ninth hour Jesus cried out with a loud voice, saying, "Eloi, Eloi, lama sabachthani?" which is translated, "My God, My God, why have You forsaken Me?" (Mark 15:34; Matthew 27:46).

JESUS' SUFFERING AND DEATH PROVOKED THE MOST POIGNANT QUESTION EVER ASKED

Why would God forsake the Sinless One? What possible reason could warrant his rejection? What purpose could it serve? Why did he receive what a child of the Devil deserves?

Jesus experienced what Scripture described as a sinner's death. Cursed under the law and cut off from God, words are insufficient to describe the awfulness of it. One so beautiful, holy, and obedient received what is reserved for profane rebels who curse God all their lives! For the first time, the Father's love was beyond Jesus' reach. Ever conscious of–Abba, Daddy's love, the Son had gazed in constant love at his Father's face, but now his Father hides his face from him. Could anything hurt more?

Twenty-one verses follow Christ's cry of forsakenness. They graphically describe his desolation: 'They strip me of my clothes and pierce my hands and my feet while people mock, accuse, and revile me. My body dehydrates. My bones are out of joint. My heart melts within me. My tongue sticks to the roof of my mouth. I count all my bones. They look and stare at me. My God, I cry out to you for answers in the morning, and in the evening I'm not silent, so why don't you answer me? Why do you do nothing? Why are you so far from helping me, and from the words of my roaring? You lay me in the dust of death. Yet, all my life I have served you.'[40]

Jesus' cry reverberates throughout creation. It is the heart-wrenching scream of the outcast, who feel forsaken by God, made desolate and empty. Jesus' suffering did not pass without him tasting fully of our loss-ness, and it was the influence of that toxic drink that shattered his heart. He felt all the dreadful feelings that accompany wretchedness. That tonic was worse than the demonic onslaught he endured, for it contained that awful ingredient that you and I have only ever felt in our very worse state of sin and shame.

Jesus' derelict cry is a window into how loss we were and how great God's redeeming love is. The Father loves you as much as he loves Jesus. He never stopped loving Jesus, but he delivered Jesus up that he may embrace you and I (John 10:17; 17:23). Our salvation was not possible unless God dealt justly with our sin, satisfied his innate holiness, justified sinners, and delivered them from Satan's domain. Christ descended into the abyss that we might ascend with him.[41] That final dimension of our deliverance helps me appreciate how horrendous that cup–once you realize the power that Satan exerted over humanity due to the depth of our rebellion.

Not only did the Son suffer, but the Father suffered. Abraham ached when he lifted that knife to offer up Isaac. For the more you love someone, the greater the anguish in watching them die—and the Father loved his son and watched him writhe in pain and heard his derelict cry. He had been the apple of his eye since before time began, but now, the separating pains of death pierced the Godhead.   Surely, the Father like Jesus endured the cross for the joy set before him (John 10:30; Hebrews 12:2).

"Yet it pleased the Lord to bruise Him." But the context is clear. It pleased him because *"the pleasure of the Lord shall prosper in His hand."* That pleasure was *"My righteous Servant shall justify many, for He shall bear their iniquities. Therefore, I will divide Him a portion*

with the great... Because He poured out His soul unto death" (Isaiah 53:10-12). A shallow reading of Isaiah fails to take into account a hundred verses that teach Jesus and his Father are one. It also discounts a multitude of places in the Bible where God grieves and suffers in his heart. *(Genesis 6:6; Isaiah 63:9; Hosea chapters 10-11; Ephesians 4: 30; 1 Corinthians 7:11; Romans 9:1-4).*

The heart of our heavenly Father is like that of an earthly father. His tender mercies and pity are aroused for his suffering child. Just as our sympathies are pulled upon in matching force to the extent to which we love someone. The greater the misery the more the compassion. Even so, Christ bearing our sin and suffering our death evokes God's compassion and spends the full extent of his wrath against sinners. If you want to know what God is like, look at Jesus, dying your death, because if you have seen him, you have seen God the Father *(John 14:7-9).*

JESUS' ASKED HIS FATHER WHY SO THAT WE MIGHT NOT MISS THE REASON HE DIED

Jesus' derelict cry was for us and it highlighted our darkness: *"Now when the sixth hour had come, there was darkness over the whole land until the ninth hour.... 'My God my God why...' Some of those who stood by, when they heard that, said, 'Look, He is calling for Elijah!'"* *(Mark 15:33-35).*

We can fail to see profound Biblical truths due to our dimness. Given the flawed and confused responses to my video trailer for Blindsided on asking God why questions, if it wasn't Jesus asking why, some might want to reprove the person who dare ask God such a direct question. If our previous five chapter do not prove that such questions are acceptable, and Jesus doing so when he died our death nothing will. There then remains for them darkness over the terrain of the cross and the Christian experience of suffering. But if we look again, we will see bright light.

But in that day, darkness over the land befits the environment of the Messiah's death. Darkness obscured the scene, so that those at the cross did not know who it was who hung there and what was happening. Christ also spoke in a language that many did not understand. They thought he cried out for Elijah to rescue him. To this day, the landscape of suffering for many remains dark. Its language, Jesus voiced from the cross, is obscure, even among Christians. They consider it a foreign state to their status as believers and interpret such cries as prayers for Elijah's miracle ministry to come rescue them. But God does not always rescue us from suffering *(Hebrews 11:35-40).*

Initially, everyone missed the message of the cross, friends and foes alike. The cross blindsided them. Yet, the reason why the Messiah suffered and died was spelled out in the Scriptures that they read every Sabbath. But they only saw Messiah's glory. They could not imagine the Messiah crying out and asking God why he had forsaken him. That was unimaginable. He was God's Chosen One. But he was also the Stone the builders rejected.

The answer to why God abandoned Jesus was there all along. It resounds even louder than the question. Thus, the Psalm that starts with the deepest question ever asked in creation, hidden from past generations, ends with an answer for all coming generations to ponder: *"You have answered me" (Psalm 22:22)*

Christ knew the reason why he would be forsaken. He asked the question so that all who follow might know. God heard Christ's cry and continues to answer him and all who would come afterwards as to why the Savior suffered and died. God will redeem mankind through his suffering, and all the ends of the earth will turn to God. Multitudes will be saved, even those who have died and those who have not yet been born. *"They will come and declare His righteousness to a people who will be born, that He has done this" (Psalm 22:22–31).*

God doesn't remain silent. He answers. You and I find all our answers in Jesus' death and resurrection. *"For He has not despised nor abhorred the affliction of the afflicted; nor has He hidden His face from Him; but when He cried to Him, He heard"* (Psalm 22:24). It appeared as if the Father turned away from Jesus as he hung on the cross, but the truth of the matter is that the Father forever looks steadfastly at what his Son accomplished there for you and me. There he redeemed us and granted us everlasting life.

"In a flood of fury I hid My face from you for a moment, But with ever-lasting lovingkindness I will have compassion on you," Says Yahweh your Redeemer" (Isaiah 54:8 Legacy Standard Bible).

An artist at his easel painted in an open-air market. It was his way of sharing his faith. As he put the final brush strokes on his painting of the crucifixion, he noticed a small girl staring at his work. After a few moments, her little face looked up at him and she solemnly said, "He must have been a very bad man to be punished that way!" The painter gently replied, "Not at all, my child. He was the best man who ever lived!"

F.J. Huegel wrote, "The cross of Calvary marked the greatest hour in the entire moral history of Deity."[42] There, God revealed his nature as holy love. What he had declared to Moses when he showed him his glory: *God hates sin but loves sinners.*

Therefore, he chooses to bear the penalty himself rather than you and I facing the final consequences of our rebellion. God satisfied his own holy justice and expressed His great loving-kindness in one great substitutionary sacrifice. It is there that the glory of God shines in the face of Jesus. It is there that God wins our love. It is there that he displays both his wisdom in dealing with sin, and his power in binding the evil of the Devil. The cross effects all of creation forever. That is the most wonderous story God has painted in all of creation.

Christ sums up this our collective story in the most basic terms: *"Was it not necessary for the Christ to suffer these things and to enter into His glory?" (Luke 24:26).* We must never lose sight of the plot: suffering before glory, going down before going up, pain before gain, thorns before thrones, crosses before crowns, and death before resurrection. This is his-story, yours, and mine. Through the centuries, it repeats itself again and again with equal fury.

So, we must hear it again and again lest we forget. It is the story of the Bible. The story of Abraham before his laughter-- Isaac, Joseph before his ascension in Egypt, Moses in the wilderness before the Exodus, Ruth before Jesse, David fleeing from Saul before he was made king, the prophets persecuted before their writing were immortalized, and ultimately Jesus rejected by his own people before every knee bow, and every tongue confesses he is Lord.

You need to get God's story right lest you lose heart. God is not punishing you. He's bringing you into a deeper communion with himself and others to himself. When you get the story right, you can take captive the Devil's lies and take courage in your losses. Whatever you have lost, you can count as gain. The voices of strangers you can ignore and let Jesus answer your every question. Your disappointments are divine appointments.

James Arthur wrote a song, *Everybody's Asking Questions.* The lyrics are moving: "Could I be the voice you turn to when you can't share your thoughts out loud... Everybody's asking questions. But I just want to talk to you. Oh, let me take all this pain from your eyes. All the feelings and feelings we felt all our lives... Let me take these voices away... Everybody keeps on talking. But I just wanna answer you."[43]

PRINCIPLES FROM

JESUS
ASKING GOD WHY

- Asking questions is something Jesus did more than all those before him.
- Asking questions for Jesus was typically not a way to get new information that he did not possess, but a means to making his point clearer and applying it more strongly.
- Asking God if it were possible that he not drink of "this cup" was not a request to avoid dying on the cross, but a prayer to not experience the forsakenness of becoming sin.
- Asking God "why have you forsaken me" shows it is alright for you to ask God why when you don't understand why you are going through the pain of loss.
- Asking "why have you forsaken me" points to profound truths that apply to you in your participation with Christ in his death.
- Asking God why as we have seen in the Old Testament also reveals the role of sin, of this evil age, of the Devil, and of others in the things that you suffer.
- Asking 'why have you forsaken me' was a forsakenness that Jesus alone experienced when he died on the cross, and it is a depth of forsakenness that you will never know because by God's grace Jesus tasted death for you.

JESUS' "WHY?" SUMMARIZED

Jesus' prayer, *"Let this cup pass from me"* was not a request to avoid the pain of crucifixion and the great indignities he would endure at the hands of sinners. The cup represents a far more dreadful experience. His soul, fully man, would experience a potion so strong that only one who was fully God and a sinless man could drink without it destroying him.

"This cup" was the source of Jesus' passion. His *"why"* question and the answer he received is also your inevitable question for God and his answer to you. We all crave the relief that answers afford. Jesus asked God why he was forsaken? He knew the answer, but his question revealed the extend of what he had to go through so that you might be made right with God. His forsakenness also limits the extent of whatever you might possibly endure this side of heaven for in making you righteous he will never leave you or forsake you.

Christ's sacrificial love, the laying down of His life for you, is the greatest act of love possible. Self-sacrifice for another, entering their pain to save them, is agape love demonstrated. At the cross, Jesus went beyond empathy and experienced what it would mean to be lost so you and I could be found in God, never to be lost again nor ever to expereince what that feels like.

Christ's death and resurrection will answer the great questions you face in life. When you understand the plot of his-story, you now have the context to appreciate why you are going through what you are going through. You also have confidence to overcome whatever comes your way.

Christ's love for you working by faith never fails to overcome. By participating in his death, God also imparts the greatest virtue possible–agape love. In defining love, the first thing Scripture says about this kind of love is that *"love suffers long . . . bears all things . . . endures all things" (1 Corinthians 13:4–7).*

So when you experience what the wicked should experience, Jesus knows how you feel. He is your faithful High Priest. He is touched by your pain, weaknesses, and temptations, and he makes intercession for you *(Hebrews 2:17-28; 4:14-16)*. Notwithstanding, unlike what Jesus experienced when he suffered, you will never be abandoned by God.

Many have suffered because they love God and others. Jeremiah was persecuted because he spoke God's truth to his neighbors. Moses also endured the rebellion of a whole nation as sought their good. Habakkuk felt a deep burden and cried out to God to do something about the sin he saw in his day. Your love will also bring you suffering in one way or another.

In our final chapter, we look at the questions the apostle Paul asked God regarding his suffering. The answers Pal received reveal huge truths concerning suffering, for after Christ revealed himself to Paul on the Damascus Road, the Lord said, *"For I will show him what great things he must suffer for My name's sake" (Acts 9:16).*

CHAPTER SEVEN

PAUL FOLLOW CHRIST LIKE HE DID

Because of the Father's great redemptive purpose to recreate us and conform us to His Son's glorious image, and our need to earnestly cooperate with his transforming work in us.

The TV series Extreme Makeover was a rave. The Home Edition ran for ten years and was relaunched in 2020 on HGTV with a new team, more heartwarming stories, and gorgeous homes. But less widely known, well-intentioned gifts often became catalysts for disasters. Renovations never solved a family's underlying issue. Some were torn apart by stress, some by interpersonal conflicts, others by increased taxes. One family featured on the show, where there was a divorce, quoted an ex-husband, "The house didn't change her. She's still her plain old nasty self."[44]

You and I need more than an extreme maker. Like Saul of Tarsus who became Paul, the great apostle to the Gentiles, experienced and taught, we need to be re-created by God. New life begins on the inside and transforms our heart throughout our earthly lives.

- **First Questions: Why do that?**
- **Who is your Lord?**
- **What must you do?**

Before his conversion, Saul was traveling to Damascus to persecute Christians. His new life began when Jesus appeared to him as a light brighter than the noon day sun. Christ, true to his practice while on earth, asked Paul a question. *"Why are you persecuting me?"* Knocked to the ground and blinded by the brilliance of that light, Saul asked, *"Who are You, Lord?"* The answer to that question set in motion a complete change in Saul, revolutionizing his life and destiny. The answer to that question, *"Who are you, Lord,"* has also transformed everyone who has ever heard the Messiah's answer: *"I am Jesus."* (Acts 9:1-5).

The answer to that lordship question determined everything Saul would do for the rest of his life. *"Trembling and astonished,"* he asked, *"What must I do?" Jesus answered, "Arise, and go to the city, and it will be told you what you must do"* (Acts 9:6).

When Jesus revealed himself as the living Messiah, Paul realized that the person and mission of the Messiah was profoundly different from anything he had ever imagined. Like his fellow countrymen, had Jesus not revealed himself to Saul, he would've continued to reject his Savior. Once, Saul knew Jesus was the Messiah, the great persecutor of the Christian faith, became Paul, the great preacher of the Messiah crucified and raised to new life.

The New Testament records many details from the life of Paul, and his letters provide profound instructions on how we are to respond to Jesus' Lordship. Paul tells his fellow believers to follow him as he follows Christ. I point this out because Paul not only had that first big question: *"Who are You, Lord?"* But he had other questions that helped him cooperate with the lasting changes that God would make in his nature and character.

Christ's glorious image was God's eternal purpose for Paul and for all who would trust in Jesus. It is his will to bring many sons to glory. Therefore, simply stated, all things, before you came to believe on Christ (BC) were intended to bring you to that place of faith in him. And all things, after you believed on Christ (AD), are intended to work in such a way that they conform you to his image: *"For whom He foreknew, He also predestined to be conformed to the image of His Son, that He might be the firstborn among many brethren"* (Romans 8:29).

- **Why the Birth Pains?**

Considering the depth of our need, nothing less than a complete conversion, our final chapter looks at why we suffer, and what we need to know when we do suffer. Paul is also our example of suffering, based on Jesus' words: *"For I will shew him how great things he must suffer for my name's sake."* (Acts 9:16 KJV). Christ showed Paul great things that will significantly aid us when we suffer. We can learn many things from this transformed man.

Before investigating those things, we must experience what Paul did, which was far more than a renovation. Paul wrote, *"Whoever is a believer in Christ is a new creation. The old way of living has disappeared. A new way of living has come into existence. The old is gone, and the new has come (1 Corinthians 5:17 NOG).*[45]

Consider your former life. You were dead in sin and were by nature a child of the Devil *(Ephesians 2:1-8)*. I don't know about you, but that described me perfectly. I drank, smoked, cussed, and acted like a fool. When I started reading the Bible, I found that living the Christian life is not difficult. It is impossible. There is so much to obey. Just being a witness is difficult. And many things I read in the Bible challenged me to the core.

The first time I read: *"Be perfect as your Heavenly Father is perfect,"* I felt like Jesus' followers who asked, *"Lord who can be saved?"* *"With men."* Jesus answered, *"it is impossible but with God all things are possible" (Matthew 5:48; 19:26)*. To this day, I find I cannot live like Jesus in my own strength. Will power isn't enough; it never is. Sure, you and I need to be willing. But oh, the power to perform what we will. Only the Spirit of Christ can empower us to live like Christ. Only Christ in us can live the Christian life.

· **Why the Thorn in the Flesh?**

Transformation begins with a new birth, but sadly many Christians live like that is an end all. Not so with Paul, our example. He needed more than a Damascus Road encounter with Jesus, and his thorn in the flesh was a big part of his ongoing transformation. All scholars agree that this thorn characterized Paul's suffering. The exact nature of Paul's thorn--his suffering is uncertain.[46] There is likely a good reason that we don't know. God wanted Paul's affliction to be described in general enough terms to apply to any difficulty or suffering you may face.

Whether the thorn you struggle with today is physical, emotional, or spiritual, it is meant to serve a redemptive purpose.

Here is what Paul said about his thorn: *"And lest I should be exalted above measure by the abundance of the revelations, a thorn in the flesh was given to me, a messenger of Satan to buffet me, lest I be exalted above measure. Concerning this thing I pleaded with the Lord three times that it might depart from me. And He said to me, 'My grace is sufficient for you, for My strength is made perfect in weakness.' Therefore, most gladly I will rather boast in my infirmities, that the power of Christ may rest upon me. Therefore, I take pleasure in infirmities, in reproaches, in needs, in persecutions, in distresses, for Christ's sake. For when I am weak, then I am strong"* (2 Corinthians 12:6-10).

This suffering, we see like many kinds of suffering, involved a demonic messenger. It is helpful that we understand Satan and his demons are agents who bring suffering. But Satan cannot do whatever he likes. Paul knew God permitted it and he wanted to know why. He wanted to cooperate with God.

- **A Need to Know Why!**

Paul did not stop asking God until he got an answer. Clearly, he did not think it wrong to ask. It was said of John Hyde who went to India in 1892 to preach Christ that he would stay on his face in prayer until the answer came. That may sound presumptuous, but it drives home the point that people not only in the Bible but throughout history have sought answers from God. Although Paul asked God three times to remove his thorn-suffering, God answered him not by removing it, but empowering him to overcome it. He also explained why it was permitted.

Two reasons Paul initially cites: (1) the promotion of humility and (2) for Paul to receive God's supernatural ability. Concerning the former, Paul's old, proud sin nature had once deceived him.

He had served God in his own ability, and he knew where that led---to persecuting Christians. Also, when you and I come to Christ our old nature is not destroyed; we must put it to death.[47]

Paul discovered that the Lord's grace was all-sufficient to enable him to live like Jesus. Christ's strength would be made perfect in Paul's weaknesses. As a result, Paul learned to rely on Christ for *"when I am weak then I am strong" (2 Corinthians 12:10).*

Paul shared his answer with the Corinthians because it was sure to help them in their struggles. He started his second letter by informing them of his severe suffering in Asia. It is a very informative passage from which you can learn vital truths about why God permits his beloved children to suffer at times, and what God promises to do through suffering:

"Blessed be the God and Father of our Lord Jesus Christ, the Father of mercies and God of all comfort, who comforts us in all our tribulation, that we may be able to comfort those who are in any trouble, with the comfort with which we ourselves are comforted by God. For as the sufferings of Christ abound in us, so our consolation also abounds through Christ. Now if we are afflicted, it is for your consolation and salvation, which is effective for enduring the same sufferings which we also suffer. Or if we are comforted, it is for your consolation and salvation. And our hope for you is steadfast because we know that as you are partakers of the sufferings, so also you will partake of the consolation. For we do not want you to be ignorant, brethren, of our trouble which came to you in Asia: that we were burdened beyond measure, above strength, so that we despaired even of life. Yes, we had the sentence of death in ourselves, that we should not trust in ourselves but in God who raises the dead, who delivered us from so great a death, and does deliver us; in whom we trust that He will still deliver us" (2 Corinthians 1:3-10).

Paul told the Corinthian about the hardships he suffered and God's purposes in allowing them. He champions God as *"the God of all comfort"* because God comforted him in all his troubles so that he could comfort others in whatever trouble they faced. That is a good reason why God allows us to suffer. Because the sufferings of Christ abounded in Paul's life, God's comfort abounded, and he was a great instrument in God's hand to bring comfort to others. Paul also learned through his suffering that he should not trust in himself but in God who raises the dead (2 *Corinthians 1:3-10; 2 Timothy 2:10; 2 Corinthians 12:6*).

- **A Need-to-Know Jesus Better!**

Paul came to realize that he personally and actively participated in the ministry of the Messiah. Isaiah predicted that the Messiah would comfort those who mourn: *"The Spirit of the Lord God is upon Me, Because the Lord has anointed Me To preach good tidings to the poor; He has sent Me to heal the brokenhearted, ... To comfort all who mourn, To console those who mourn in Zion, To give them beauty for ashes, The oil of joy for mourning, The garment of praise for the spirit of heaviness... that He may be glorified"* (*Isaiah 61:1-3 see also Isaiah 12:1; 40:1; 49:13; 51:3-12; 52:9; 57:18*).

We saw in our last chapter that Jesus bore our sorrows and carried our sickness to the cross. Yet, in following Jesus, Paul experienced the sufferings of Christ. He discovered that Christ's own death and resurrection was at work in him. And it was through Paul's vital union with his Lord that he brought comfort to those who were afflicted.

oPaul testified that God constantly delivered him and that even his physical death would be a deliverance to glorify God (*Philippians 1:20*). This is true not only for Paul but all of Jesus' followers, for Paul is a pattern and example for all who would believe in Christ (*1 Timothy 1:16; 1 Thessalonians 1:6; 1 Corinthians 11:1*).

- **A Need for Perspective!**

After years of suffering, Paul affirmed that it is only a matter of time, and our eternal rewards will far outweigh our current pain: *"For I consider that the sufferings of this present time are not worthy to be compared with the glory which shall be revealed in us"* (Romans 8:18). He deemed, *"For our light affliction, which is but for a moment, is working for us a far more exceeding and eternal weight of glory, while we do not look at the things which are seen, but at the things which are not seen. For the things which are seen are temporary, but the things which are not seen are eternal"* (2 Corinthians 4:17-18).

- **A Need to Fill What is Lacking!**

To the Colossians, Paul wrote, *"I now rejoice in my sufferings for you, and fill up in my flesh what is lacking in the afflictions of Christ, for the sake of His body, which is the church"* (Colossians 1:24–27).

The Christ that Paul preached offers the most glorious answer to suffering ever given mankind: *suffering for others demonstrates your love, bringing hope, comfort, and certain victory to all who trust God in their suffering.* In the process, you deeply participate in Jesus' life, messianic mission, death, and resurrection. Thus, you are conformed to his image, and truly become like him.

That's true not only of missionaries who suffer hardships and persecution so that others can hear and believe, but for all Christians. Every godly person will experience trouble in this world, suffer rejection, and face demonic opposition.

- **A Need to Learn Love!**

Suffering for others to know Christ is the most Christlike thing a person can do. And like the cup of water given in Jesus' name, none of it goes unnoticed by God. That willingness to suffer patiently so that others can hear and believe was lacking in Paul's day, and it is lacking even more today in our age of comfort and convenience. It is not that you or I somehow earn salvation by suffering. Paul wasn't claiming that, nor did he claim that his suffering added anything to what Jesus suffered to redeem you and me *(Hebrews 9:26)*. Paul's suffering, however, was necessary so that others could hear the message, believe, and be saved *(Romans 10:15)*.

· **A Need to be Filled with the Holy Spirit's Power!**

The power Paul received from God was not limited to being born again on Damascus Road. For we read: *"And Ananias went his way and entered the house; and laying his hands on him he said, "Brother Saul, the Lord Jesus, who appeared to you on the road as you came, has sent me that you may receive your sight and be filled with the Holy Spirit. Immediately there fell from his eyes something like scales, and he received his sight at once; and he arose and was baptized" (Acts 9:17-19)*. Paul needed the infilling power of the Holy Spirit to bring about all the changes that God desired in and through his life.

Superhuman power is essential. It's the biggest missing element in the church's life and witness. For years, I attended church without a living, active faith in Jesus. Ignorant and empty, I came to Jesus without a pa rum pa pum pum of drums to play for him. I did, however, have several friends like me who only knew about him. They were Roman Catholics and wondered what had happened to me. I struggled to tell them. I recall Chris sitting in my car, waving his hand toward the houses up and down the street. "You mean we're all wrong." I replied, "You can know for sure that you are going to heaven. There is so much more!"

It was only later that I received power to witness. My first evening at Faith Fellowship, the Pastor was preaching on the rivers of living water that flow from your inner most being.

I only knew the Catholic Mass, and I expected with the final, "Amen," a rush for the doors. I thought if I don't do something fast, I'll have to wait another week to receive this power I desperately need. I quickly raised my hand to get the pastor's attention. Everyone's head turned in my direction. "I want to be filled the Holy Spirit" I said. "Well, come to the front," Wilbur said with a smile. He laid his hand on my head, my lips quivered, and I felt a surge of power. That night I prayed for two hours like I had never prayed before. My heart was filled with love and joy beyond what I thought possible. I was so charged up. I witnessed for Jesus to everyone I met.

- **A Need to Experience the Baptism with Fire!**

Jesus not only promised to baptize us with the Holy Spirit, but with fire. That clearly speaks of suffering fiery trials as a Christ follower. Paul suffered greatly, but it is crucial to know, as he did, that God never forsakes us: *"persecuted but not abandoned" (2 Corinthians 4:9)*. When we suffer, God draws near to us with his presence and power. It is like Joseph when he was sold as a slave and imprisoned. *"The Lord was with Joseph" (Genesis 39:2). It's like the three Hebrews in the fiery furnace with "the form of the fourth is like the Son of God" (Daniel 3:25).*

- **A Need for Presence!**

You and I will never experience the forsakenness Jesus experienced when he hung on the cross, bearing the sins of the world. You will experience suffering for others, but never a sense of being cut off from God. The Lord promised he would not leave nor forsake the Israelites (Deuteronomy 31:6-7). In the New Testament, that promise to believers is emphatically stated, *"For He Himself has said, 'I will never leave or forsake you'" (Hebrews 13:6).* Jesus was forsaken on the cross so that you and I would never be forsaken. The world and others may reject you but not Christ.

- **A Need to Identify with Others!**

Paul identified with Christ and his Jewish brothers to the point
where he says, *"For I could wish that I myself were accursed (forsak-
en, cut off) from Christ for my brethren" (Romans 9:3).* He understood
their unbelief in Jesus as the Messiah because he had been one
of them. Like them, he thought he was righteous by keeping
the law of Moses. The unbelief of his brothers was his greatest
sorrow in life, but he allowed his grief to motivate him to give
his all for Christ and for them, which included suffering to reach
them with the good news of the Messiah.

When the apostles, James and John, asked for the most powerful positions in Christ's Kingdom–to sit on Jesus' right and left
hand, Jesus spoke of the necessity of drinking from the cup he
drank *(Mark 10:35-45).* That cup, as we saw last chapter speaks
of suffering. Christians who seek honor and glory as Christ
followers need to understand that those most honored in God's
Kingdom will be those who have suffered the greatest for Jesus'
name. Pride and selfish ambition have no place in the Christian
life, only humility and the well being of others.

- **A Need to Endure Suffering before Reigning!**

*"Then James and John, the sons of Zebedee, came to Him, saying,
"Teacher, we want You to do for us whatever we ask." And He said to
them, "What do you want Me to do for you?" They said to Him, "Grant
you that we may sit, one on Your right hand and the other on Your left,
in Your glory." But Jesus said to them, "You do not know what you ask.
Are you able to drink the cup that I drink, and be baptized with the
baptism that I am baptized with?" They said to Him, "We are able."
So Jesus said to them, "You will indeed drink the cup that I drink, and
with the baptism I am baptized with you will be baptized; but to sit on
My right hand and on My left is not Mine to give, but it is for those for
whom it is prepared" (Mark 10:35-40).*

In the original Greek, the question was phrased to make clear a negative answer is expected. But when James and John told Jesus they could drink his cup and endure his baptism, our Savior agreed they would, but as the original etymology indicated, Christ was not saying that they would experience being forsaken by God or that their suffering would atone for people's sin. The cup they drank did not have the same ingredients as the cup Christ drank. They did, however, share in his suffering. That cup contained all kinds of suffering that we all drink to some measure. But we never experience the sense of forsakenness Jesus did when he died our death.

- **A Need to Hear God's Whole Counsel!**

You and I can misapply certain promises in the Bible. When God doesn't do what you think he should, it can cause us to stumble. An example of misusing the Bible is what the Devil did when he tempted Jesus with the promised protection of Psalm ninety-one *(Matthew 4:5-6)*. That Psalm promises that *"No evil shall befall you" (Psalm 91:1-10)*. In a similar fashion, Jesus promised his followers, *"Nothing shall by any means hurt you" (Luke 10:19)*. Yet, he told them they would be persecuted, and some would be put to death *(Matthew 10:16-42)*. My point: *the Devil can tempt and provoke you with Bible promises that seem to fail in your life when you isolate those promises from the whole message of the Bible.*

When my son was hit and killed by an errant hammer throw, the Devil taunted me when I read Psalm ninety-one. It seemed what God promised had failed or Ethan had failed to dwell under his wings when that hammer hit him at midday. But I stopped allowing Satan to torment me as I accepted that the no harm Jesus promised his followers was harm to their souls and spirits. *"Fear not those who can harm the body" (Matthew 10:28)*. Many early saints were executed. Jesus even told Peter what kind of death Peter would die to glorify God (John 21:19).

The Bible teaches that in this present evil age, God only permits suffering at the hands of the Devil for a finite time and for a good, redemptive purpose. We saw Job suffered. But he received a double portion blessing, and God promises to fully reward you in eternity. *"If indeed we suffer with Him, that we may also be glorified together"* (Romans 8:17; 2 Timothy 2:12).

Jesus' suffering was redemptive, and God intends that your anguish serve a redeeming purpose. Not redeeming in the sense that your suffering saves you or others, but in that it serves a good, eternal purpose. That is in keeping with God promises to work all things, even evil and painful things, together for a greater good: *"And we know that all things work together for good to those who love God, to those who are the called according to His purpose"* (Romans 8:28).

· **A Need to be Assured!**

"All things work together for good" is not a trite cliché, glibly uttered. It is a life preserver. This promise helps carry your heart through the floodgates of turbulent waters. I call it, "God's Assurance Policy." Paul learned this experientially. He also saw it recorded in all the lives of God's people who went before him. And he is not saying that all things are good but that your Father is so powerful, wise, and good that He works bad things for your good. You and I have our list of bad things that God has turned around for good. And whatever may happen in your life, God assures you of his love and power to redeem it. I esteem this as the greatest promise God has given us this side of heaven.

This promise is made amidst a catalogue of the worse possible evils known to mankind: *being naked, starving, and being killed by the sword (Romans 8:36).* If that promise is true amidst the worse of life, you can trust God that you'll grow through your lesser losses in life. We certainly learn more from pain than we do from pleasure. For if God prevented pain regardless of what we did, we would become the most reckless and self-centered people imaginable. Not only do you learn obedience through the things you suffer, but you also learn compassion, gratitude, and many godly virtues that pleasure never produce *(Hebrews 5:8)*.

You and I might rather have trouble-free lives, but love and faith wouldn't grow strong that way. Hence, the only condition to qualify for the promise of Romans 8:28 is that you love God. Genuine love for God is purified by the fiery trials you endure. These trials prove your love for him, your family, and others *(James 1:12)*.

It's vital to know that nothing that will happen to you that can ever separate you from the love of God because of what God's Son did on the cross. Not only that, but if God did not spare His only Son, surely, he will freely give you all things that you need to live a life of love and faith *(Romans 8:32)*.

God's promise to use what is bad for good was fully demonstrated in Christ's death. For God used the greatest of evils, the execution of the Prince of Life, for the greatest possible good, granting eternal life to all who would trust him. God also vindicated Jesus by raising him from the dead and seating him at his right hand, enthroned with all authority and power. When Jesus returns to the earth, the dead will be raised, and all God's promise will be fulfilled to the nth degree. Our own bodily resurrection will complete the working of all things together for good.

- **A Need to Let Go and Let God!**

Meanwhile, through Christ God brings about a great exchange: good to replace evil, Jesus' life for your life, his righteousness for your sins, his faith for your doubts, his strength for your weaknesses, his hope for your despair, his thoughts and ways for your thoughts and ways, his garment of praise for your spirit of heaviness, his peace for your turmoil, his joy for your sorrow, his gentle yoke of learning his humility for your oppressive yoke of selfish pride, his resurrection for your own death, his answers for your questions, the mind of Christ for your mind, and his best out of your worst.

Think of Israel's worse. Worse than worshipping idols or trusting in other nations was her rejection of her King, Jesus. What Paul writes in Romans chapter nine, thus, connects logically to God's redemptive purpose for Israel despite her rejection of Christ. Paul explains this in chapters nine to eleven. For as a Hebrew of Hebrews, it was extremely painful for Paul to see his country-men reject Jesus. It created a huge why question for Paul. But he shares the answer God gave him concerning Israel's apostasy:

"I tell the truth in Christ, I am not lying, my conscience also bearing me witness in the Holy Spirit, that I have great sorrow and continual grief in my heart. For I could wish that I myself were accursed from Christ for my brethren, my countrymen according to the flesh, who are Israelites, to whom pertain the adoption, the glory, the covenants, the giving of the law, the service of God, and the promises; of whom are the fathers and from whom, according to the flesh, Christ came, who is over all, the eternally blessed God. Amen" (Romans 9:1-5).

- **A Need to Focus on the Ending!**

The Jewish people are central to God's story. Their history is intricately tied to the story of God. God created the world and placed man in it. Mankind, sins, and death enter the world. God promises a Saving Seed to deliver man. That Seed will bless all families of the earth and he will come through Abraham's offspring. They are enslaved by the Egyptians, but dramatical-ly delivered by God. They become the nation of Israel and are given God's law by Moses. Their prophets continue to predict the coming Messiah. He will usher in God's glorious kingdom's reign. They long for his coming but fail to recognize him when he comes. Worse still, he is rejected by them and handed over to their enemies, the Gentiles. Following Israel's rejection of Christ, their magnificent temple is destroyed, and they are driven out of the land God gave them. They are persecuted and scattered among the nations. But God is not done with them.

The Israeli people, though willful in their rejection of Christ and accountable to God for it, are a case in point of God working this great evil together for good. In Romans chapter nine, Paul unpacks God's redemptive answer concerning Israel's rejection of Jesus as Messiah and explains God's purpose in allowing this to happen. It a multi-faceted answer

The answer God gave Paul begins with *"they are not all Israel who are of Israel" (Romans 9:6)*. The Old Testament Scriptures testified to the fact repeatedly that individual Israelites can be cut off from the nation. Many were. A whole generation perished in the wilderness and failed to enter the Promised Land because of unbelief. God's selection of people, Paul explains, separates believing individuals to himself and cuts off those who disbelieve. This is according to his justice *(Romans 9:14)*.

Not all Israel is Israel also points to the fact that individually some Israelites are born of his Spirit, and others are born after the flesh. This was not only true for Abraham's sons Isaac in contrast to Ishmael, but also true of Isaac's sons, Jacob and Esau, and all the generations that followed. For this great truth, Paul cites the frequent Old Testament doctrine of a remnant and refers to believers as children of promise *(Romans 9:6-13, 27-29)*.

In Romans chapter nine, Paul maintains that God, being a sovereign creator and redeemer, has the right to have mercy on whom he will have mercy *(Romans 9:15-26)*. God saves people by faith and not by the works of the law because under the law all stand condemned *(Romans 9:30-10:21)*. God's purpose was always to have mercy upon all for all, have sinned and are guilty of disobedience *(Romans 11:30-36)*.

Paul was told that God had not forsaken Israel; there is a remnant, a grafting back in of those Israelites who believe in Jesus as Messiah, and an end-time revival of redemption among them *(Romans 11:1-10, 23 29)*. This has begun as the fullness of the Gentiles come to Christ and the nation Israel has returned to the promise land. God's ways are perfect in wisdom and knowledge, and beyond human scrutiny *(Romans 11:33-36)*.

As a people group, Israel participates in God's story. He even uses their rejection of Jesus to bring mercy to believers from all the nations. Akin to Jesus' death, God has worked it together for the good of mankind. He has created one new, united body of people, the church.

Paul speaks of this mystery revealed to him and sums up its ramifications, instructing the Gentiles to humility and sobriety: *"Concerning the gospel, they are enemies for your sake, but concerning the election, they are beloved for the sake of the fathers. For the gifts and the calling of God are irrevocable. For as you were once disobedient to God, yet have now obtained mercy through their disobedience, even so these also have now been disobedient, that through the mercy shown you they also may obtain mercy. For God has committed them all to disobedience, that He might have mercy on all. Oh, the depth of the riches both wisdom and knowledge of God! How unsearchable are His judgments and His ways past finding out!" (Romans 11:28-33)*.

Paul found great comfort in God's answer concerning his countrymen. For the death of the Messiah had blindsided the Jewish people. Even Christ's initial disciples were blindsided by it. On the Emmaus Road, the disciples failed to recognize Jesus because they did not understand the storyline from the Law, the Prophets, and the Writings.

· **A Need to Put Yourself in the Story!**

Jesus had to explain the story to his followers on the Emmaus Road: Abraham and Sarah endured the heartache of barrenness before their Isaac was born. "Everything is against me!" Jacob exclaimed before he discovered that Joseph was still alive. Righteous Job lost his children, his wealth, and his health before God restored double to him. Moses spent forty years in a desert before he delivered Israel out of Egypt. David fled for his life from Saul's javelin before he reigned over Israel as king. God's messengers, the prophets, were all rejected before their writings were immortalized. It's all one story. God uses the very things they suffer to bring them to glory. And Paul provides an amazing overview of suffering. For love's sake, God allows people to choose what they will believe and do, which permits various short-term evils. But God promises he will forever overrule evil for the good of those who trust and obey him.

· **A Need to be Reminded!**

Like the saints of old, you and I need to be reminded of the story we share, lest we miss the plot. *"You meant evil against me; but God meant it for good, in order to bring it about as it is this day, to save many people alive." "So now it was not you who sent me here but God"* (Genesis 45:8; 50:20). God used the bad will of Joseph's brothers to bring about his good will. They were responsible for their jealousy and betrayal, and although God hated their lies and discord, he did not intervene, because he intended to work it all together for good and redeem them.

God's promises are always bigger and better than you have imagined. When you think God's promise has failed, he has something bigger and better planned. The Davidic Covenant appeared fail when Israel no longer had an ancestor of David sitting on an earthly throne in Jerusalem. That failure was because of sin, but God still had a bigger and better fulfillment than David could've ever imagined. The Messiah would sit on David's throne forever, over all of mankind, and a new race of creatures, recreated in his glorious image, in a New Jerusalem with streets of gold, on a New Earth in a New Heaven, where they would see and serve God face to face.

PRINCIPLES FROM
PAUL
ASKING GOD WHY

- Asking God, "Who are you, Lord?" activated Paul's eternal destiny and shaped the entire course of western civilization and world history.
- Asking God what must I do like Paul asked shows our willingness to participate in Jesus' Messianic ministry.
- Asking God why he allowed a messenger of Satan to buffet him taught Paul that God's all sufficient grace was made perfect in his weaknesses, and God given answers to your suffering can do the same for you.
- Asking God why he suffered led Paul to understand that his life was an intimate participation in the life, ministry, death, and resurrection of Jesus Christ.
- Asking God questions in faith empowered Paul, and he is given by God as a pattern and example for all believers.
- Asking God questions provided Paul and you with an amazing answer that we are called to co-labor with Christ.
- Asking God why helped Paul experience and articulate God's great promise to "work all things together for good" for those who love him.

PAUL'S "WHY?" SUMMARIZED

When you suffer, God calls you to trust him. For he only permits you to hurt for a season, and he decided in advance that whatever pain you experience will bring about a lasting good, which would never have existed otherwise, but will now continue forever. There is, therefore, no better world God could create. The world you presently live in allows you the capacity to love freely and to choose to trust God explicitly. Freedom allowed for evil, but our sovereign God commands all things to serve his eternal, redemptive purposes that ultimately work to bring about what is good.

You and me like Paul find the ultimate answer to our deepest why God questions in the good news of Christ: *Did the devil instigate Jesus' death? You bet. Was it evil? No greater evil ever perpetrated on earth! Did God allow it? Absolutely! Did he hold Judas, the Sanhedrin, and Pilate responsible? Certainly! Did good come out of it? No greater good possible than the redemption of all who would believe it. God's reign brings the good news of Christ's suffering and dying, rising, and ascending to the Father's right hand, and coming again to resurrect the dead and restore his creation.*

The suffering you experience as God's child will bring you, like it did Paul, into the closest fellowship with Jesus possible. So, you can identify with your Lord: *his sacrificial love, his humble heart, his deep empathy, his confident relationship to his Father, his wise means of overcoming evil with good, and every beautiful facet of his nature! As a result, you can experience his higher order of good: faith, hope, and love, which are not possible without free will and obstacles to overcome.*

In concluding, I borrow an expression from the nineteen century: 'mind your Ps and Qs!'[48] When we talk of suffering, Qs equal Questions, and Ps, Principles. I pray the principles provided when we have questions will serve us well. In closing, I offer a final shortlist of ten Ps when you or someone you love suffers.

SCRIPTURE
WHEN YOU SUFFER

Paul – followed in the steps of Jesus and his life is given to believers as an example of various generic reasons why Christians suffer.

Providence – Scripture affirms that God rules over his creation, and he permits evil things to happen, even as common as the falling of a sparrow from the sky.

Purpose – God has a good redemptive purpose in the suffering he allows to occur.

Partnership and Participation – the believer's life is a participation in the life, ministry, death, and resurrection of Jesus the Messiah.

Pain – don't waste your pain, for it is a great source of learning and motivation from which you can minister faith, comfort, and assurance to others, especially those who are currently suffering.

Personal – suffering is deeply personal, only fully known and understood by Jesus, God's Suffering Servant.

Perspective – God doesn't answer our why questions about why others have suffered to satisfy our curiosity, but only those that aim to cooperate with him and have a vested interest in knowing.

Principlalities and Powers – evil spirit, what the Bible calls demons, or messengers of Satan are often the agents and source of suffering.

Promise – God makes a wonderful promise in the Bible to those who suffer and one of the greatest this side of heaven is that God will work all things together for our good, particularly our suffering.

Perspective – there are many principles of suffering, and the list of ten outlined below provides a helpful resource on suffering.

PETER'S FIRST LETTER
ON SUFFERING

1. Suffering in various forms, whether in your body and/or soul (1:6,11; 2:4,12,19; 3:9,14-17; 4:1,14-16) originated with Satan's rebellion (5:8), and during this present evil age suffering happens to all Christian in every part of the world (5:9); yet, suffering is always subject to God's will–redemptive purposes (3:17; 4:19), and limited by Him in scope and time (5:10).

2. Suffering can be prepared for by gaining a clear understanding of the purposes for which God allows it so that when suffering comes you can overcome it by faith and love (4:1-3; 4:12).

3. Suffering may (2:20; 3:17) or may not be (2:19-21-24; 3:14-17; 4:15) for sins personally committed.

4. Suffering death in the person of Jesus was God's way of redeeming you from sin (1:11,18-20; 3:18; 4:1) as the Second Person of the Triune Godhead paid your full penalty.

5. Suffering is used by God to cause sin to cease (4:1-3), to move you closer to God (2:18-23; 3:13), to overcome evil with good (3:9-12), to bring others to faith in Christ (2:12-15; 3:18) to demonstrate, via perseverance, Jesus' Lordship in your life (3:15), to restore, mature, strengthen, and complete you (5:10).

6. Suffering for what is right is a powerful way to glorify God (4:16), as Jesus exemplified (2:21-23), and it brings blessings (3:14), including the Spirit of glory in your life (4:14; 1:7-8; 4:13; 5:1,4,10), and therefore you mustn't be fearful or ashamed when you suffer as though you did something wrong (3:6,13-14; 4:16).

7. Suffering enables you to sympathize with others who are suffering and to minister comfort and encouragement to those who suffer (5:9).

8. Suffering is part of your story (1:6-9,11;4:12-14;5:9), an intimate participation in Christ's suffering (4:13).

9. Suffering qualifies you to reign with Christ (5:10) by testing the genuineness of your faith in God and love for Him like gold is purified in the fire (1:7-9).

10. Suffering in this present evil age is not worthy to be compared with the glory you will receive in the coming age and that age is without end (5:4).

The entire Bible provides a framework for interpreting and over-coming suffering. From the first day you suffer to the day God glorifies it, he has a good purpose and foolproof plan for allowing it. God may or may not show you specific answers as to why you are suffering. If he does reveal a reason, it will, when properly interpreted, agree with what the Bible teaches. It will also help you endure and overcome what you suffer. God is walking with you and often talking to you so you can cooperate with what he plans to do. He promises that all things, even the very things that seem dead set against you, like suffering in your body and/or soul, will become the very things that God uses for your good.

PRAYER OF COMMITTED TRUST

Dear Lord,
You are holy and just. I desire to know why You allowed this (fill in with your situation) to happen to me. I ask to know why in order that I might cooperate with your purposes. Lord, I give you my emotion(s) (fill in whatever emotions you are experiencing such as disappointment, anger, grief etc....). Lord, I ask based on my covenant relationship with you through your Son Jesus who died for my sins and lives to make intercession for me. Lord, I love you and want to glorify you, so I ask with a humble heart that is willing to receive whatever answer You give me. If you decide to be silent, I will still love and obey you. I do believe whatever you allow; you allow for a redemptive purpose and that you will bring good out of it. You alone have the power and right to determine if this (fill in with your situation) should have been allowed to happen. Your will to act or not act is up to you, and I acknowledge that you do not have to explain yourself to me for me to trust in you and to love you. I believe you love me no matter what happens to me and to those I love. But I also believe you hear me and will answer me, for I see that is what you do in your Word, your revealed will. Thank you, that my questions and your answers will help me and not hinder me in serving you according to all your good purposes. Thank you for your Word, that gives wisdom and understanding of your ways. Thank you for giving me the Holy Spirit to guide into all the truth and for revealing your thoughts to me, even the deep things of your Spirit. Thank you also for giving me the mind of Christ. AMEN!

Endnotes

1 Hagstrom, Anders. "Police searching for home of Texas shooter where he lived with parents: report," Fox News May 7, 2023, https://www.foxnews.com/us/police-searching-home-texas-shooter-where-he-lived-parents-report.

2 Merriam Webster Dictionary , s.v. "Why," https://www.merriam-webster.com/dictionary/why

3 The Cleansing of the Heavens, God's Sovereignty, The Unsealed Book, My Africa Dream, Blindsided available at www.mcroser.com

4 Questions of why are at times rhetorical questions—to make a point. (Genesis 26:27; 27:45; 31:27-30; 42:1; 47:15-19). We'll not look at the rhetorical use of why, nor when it is asked concerning the motives of others.

5 "Why There Is Anything at All." 2020. Wikipedia. August 5, 2020. https://en.wikipedia.org/wiki/Why_there_is_anything_at_all

6 The Global Religious Landscape | Pew Research Center.

7 A sense of morality, that is the law written within human hearts, is a proof of God as the only existential basis of what is good and evil.

8 Where two or more incidents occur without an obvious casual connection between them.

9 Meacham, Jon (2013). Thomas Jefferson: The Art of Power. New York: Random House p. 496. As a result, their timely deaths did not go unnoticed. John Quincy called the coincidence of their deaths on the nation's jubilee anniversary "visible and palpable remarks of Divine Favor." Many might dispute that interpretation, but few would deny its strangeness.

10 The exodus of Israel from Egypt is a type of our deliverance from all the tests, temptations, troubles, and traumas of the world by which we come to know the Lord.

11 That is what real leaders primarily do for the people they lead

12 The Serpent in Eden with a question, questioned God's character (Genesis 3:4-5). Habakkuk 1:1-2:20

13 Notice all the question in Habakkuk 1:1-2:20.

14 Lewis, Clive S. The Problem of Pain. 2014. Reprint, New York, NY: Harpercollins, 2015.

15 Why Did God Allow This to Happen? by Greg Laurie on Oct 2, 2017

16 God disciplines all nations and individual. In 70AD, God also used pagan Rome to punish the Jewish nation for its rejection of their Messiah. God's principle in creation of sowing and reaping applies to individuals and nations. Those who sow to their sinful nature will reap death from their evil actions. But God's desire is to have mercy on all and to bring his salvation to all nation as he promised through Abraham.

17 If a child can ask a flawed parent their questions, you and I can surely ask our perfect, heavenly Father the questions we have? He is more patient than any earthly parent, and he knows the answer to everything (Matthew 7:11).

18 In Sodom, God rescued a righteous man, named Lot, whose soul "was vexed as he saw and heard their filthy way of life" (2 Peter 2:7-8).

19 Leviticus 18:21 ESV reads, "You shall not give any of your children to offer them to Molech, and so profane the name of your God: I am the Lord."

20 Lincoln's Second Inaugural Address.

21 "And as for this house, which is exalted, everyone who passes by it will be astonished and will hiss, and say, 'Why has the Lord done thus to this land and to this house?' Then they will answer, 'Because they forsook the Lord their God, who brought their fathers out of the land of Egypt, and have embraced other gods, and worshiped them and served them; therefore the Lord has brought

all this calamity on them'" (1 Kings 9:8-9).

22 Almost a whole Israelite tribe, Benjamin, was wiped out and they cried out to God. "O Lord God of Israel, why has this come to pass in Israel, that today there should be one tribe missing in Israel?" (Judges 21:3) Again, it was because of sin.

23 BBC Business News January 13, 2022 "The people using YouTube to pay for their French chateau."

24 Bildad confronted Job with these strong words, "For though I were righteous, I could not answer Him; I would beg mercy of my Judge.... If I am wicked, woe to me; Even if I am righteous, I cannot lift up my head. I am full of disgrace; See my misery!" (Job 9:14;10:15).

25 The Pharisees said to the blind man Jesus healed, "You were completely born in sins, and are you teaching us?" They did not like him telling them, Jesus could not have done the miracle unless God was with him (John 9:34)

26 This is not to say that Jesus taught that sin is never the answer to suffering. To another man, Jesus said, "See, you have been made well. Sin no more, lest a worse thing come upon you." (John 5:14).

27 A study of fear in Job bears out that his fear was the reverential fear of the Lord that is the beginning of wisdom and leads to godly living (Job 1:1,8-9; 2:3; 3:25; 4:14; 6:14; 9:35; 11:15; 15:4; 21:9; 22:4,10; 25:2; 28:28; 33:7; 37:24; 39:22; 41:33).

28 Blindsided: A Journey from Tragic Loss to Triumph Love, Paraclete Press, Copyright 2021, available at www.mcroser.com

29 First Do No Harm, 1997 American made-for-television drama-film directed by Jim Abrahams about a boy whose severe epilepsy, unresponsive to medications with terrible side effects, is controlled by the ketogenic diet. Aspects of the story mirror Abrahams' own experience with his son Charlie who suffered greatly at the hands of doctors when there was a known homeopathic treatment-diet that had helped many children. The film starts Meryl Streep (Actor), Fred Ward (Actor), Rated: PG-13.

30 In the Book of Job, the word "answer" appears nearly seventy times.

31 The decline in church attendance in the USA has continued unabated. Christianity Today: Why 9/11 Brought Neither Unity Nor Revival by Bonnie Kristian, September 10, 2021. Faith After the Pandemic: How COVID-19 Changed American Religion By Daniel A. Cox | Jennifer Benz | Lindsey Witt-Swanson. Survey Center on American Life, January 05, 2023.

32Studies show that people who ask questions have higher emotional intelligence and a greater understanding of the world around them — plus, people like them more because they are showing an interest in them. By Aytekin Tank September 7, 2021.

33 Harvard Business Review January 8, 2021of the book "Good Leadership Is About Asking Good Questions" by John Hagel III.

34 Jesus knew questions were wonderful opportunities to train, increasing the likelihood of their retention of a life lesson. Today, many still hold that questions are a key to all learning.

35 "Why do you ask Me? Ask those who have heard Me what I said to them. Indeed they know what I said" (John 18:21)

36 The Douay-Rheims 1899 American Edition.

37 https://www.biblegateway.com/ Ezekiel 23:33.

38 Ezekiel 23:33 The Message: The Bible in Contemporary Language is a translation of the Bible in contemporary English. Authored by Eugene H. Peterson and published in segments from 1993 to 2002.

39 The Voice translation: "This is the cup of ruination, of destruction." Easy-to-Read Version render desolation as "destruction." The New International Readers Version "The cup of my anger will completely destroy you." The New King James "the cup of dismay and desolation."

40 My own paraphrase of Psalm 22:1-21.

41 The Scripture clearly teaches that Jesus descended in hell (1 Peter 3:19; Ephesians 4:19; Hosea 13:14; Acts 2:24).

42 Calvary's Wondrous Cross by F.J. Huegel, 1949, out of print, limited availability.

43 James Arthur - Everybody's Asking Questions Song Lyrics, Know the Words.

44 The List, Entertainment, Extreme Makeover, Home Edition Stories that End in Tragedy, by Fiama Mastrangel, October 2021.

45 The Names of God Bible (NOG), Baker House, 2011 transliterates original language names of God.

46 Scholars cite Galatians 4:13-15 where the Galatians would have given Paul their eyes. Poor eyesight they claim forced him to dictate his letters or in the case of the Galatians use large size letters. (Gal. 6:11). They cite Acts 23:1-5 as an example of his poor eyesight when he looked intently at the Sanhedrin and failed to recognize the High Priest. Some claim his eyesight suffered after he was blinded by the light of Jesus, and his healing was not total. Others claim his eyes may have suffered from many beatings and a stoning. Some claim the 'thorn in the flesh' is simply a descriptive term which he employed to describe a host of things he was called to suffer for the cause of Christ, which are listed in 2 Corinthians 11:23ff. They cite Paul's use of the term thorn in his side, which is first used in Joshua 23:13 and again in Judges 2:3 and refers to a host of adversaries that inflicted many physical infirmities.

47 Galatians 1:13-14 compare with 1 Corinthians 12:7

48 Although the origin of the expression is debated, the best explanation favors a literal interpretation, regarding possible confusion between the lowercase letters p and q in schoolwork. For when pupils were taught the lowercases in the alphabet, the position of the vertical line before or after the circle represented different letters: d & b, p & q. Pupils also had to mind the order of letters in the alphabet—p comes before q. (The Oxford English Dictionary in 2007 agrees that this must be the true origin of the phrase. Mind your Ps and Qs Wikipedia The Free Encyclopedia).

OTHER BOOKS
BY MARK

AVAILABLE AT WWW.MCROSER.COM

Blindsided:
A Journey from Tragic Loss to Triumphant Love
(Companion book with They Asked Why)

Blindsided offers God size answers to life's biggest questions! If you ever wondered why something hurtful has happened, you need to read his story. It is an intense, grief narrative driven by 'the why God question.' But it is also a story of profound discovery. Ethan Roser died during a college track and field accident. Mark wrote to process his grief. Little did he know how God would give him and my family real life, biblical, answers. God size answers. Those answers not only apply to his son's death, but to many young lives that seem tragically cut short, and they promote a deeper trust in God when we experience deep loss.

Blindsided has great appeal for people of faith who believe that God is intimately involved in their lives. And because God is sovereign, they wonder why tragedy strikes, whether questions are verbalized or not. Hurting people always look for answers. Mark's story provides answers for you and your neighbors, whose ears you will have when tragedy strikes, answers that will help them turn to God and cooperate with his redemptive purposes.

Blindsided was also written for people who reckon that things happen by mere chance; yet they are unsure of their agnosticism. Mark's theological studies, a doctorate in Biblical studies, and his practical experiences, twenty-plus years in Africa, help himaddress the question of why.

My African Dream:
Transformed by the Rain

Inspiring and challenging memoir from Mark and Pat Roser documenting their adventures over the past thirty years in war torn Zimbabwe. From colonialism to poverty, war, dictators and AIDS, this beautifully documented story will change your view of the world and your place in it.

God's Sovereignty:
Trust God More

The comfort and wonder of an all-powerful, all-knowing, ever-present God, directing the affairs of this life, is all but lost in our secular society. We need new thoughts concerning the infinite, majesty of God. What do you believe? Do you believe that bad things just happen to people? Or do you believe that there is not a single event that can occur outside of God's sovereign control? This book will help you trust God.

The Unsealed Book:
A Study of the Book of Revelation

A comprehensive study of the Book of Revelation, written so all can understand it. Covers the five major views, has tremendous stories to illustrate, and answers crucial questions, providing a consistent Biblical interpretation. It's a great resource for small group studies includes discussion questions for each chapter.

The Cleansing of the Heavens:
The Accuser Cast Down

Can Satan accuse us before God like Job? Has the Devil's position changed from Old to New Testament? When and why? What difference does it make? Dr. Peter Wagner writes: "I began saying, 'Wait a minute! I am reading things that I have never read or heard before!' Questions such as what immediate influence the cross of Christ might have had on the modus operandi of Satan in the unseen realms.